THE JOY
OF MOVEMENT
IN EARLY CHILDHOOD

Early Childhood Education Series

MILLIE ALMY, EDITOR

Elinor Fitch Griffin, *Island of Childhood: Education in the Special World of Nursery School*

Sandra Curtis, *The Joy of Movement in Early Childhood*

THE JOY
OF MOVEMENT
IN EARLY CHILDHOOD

SANDRA R. CURTIS

University of California, Berkeley

Teachers College, Columbia University
New York and London, 1982

Published by Teachers College Press, 1234 Amsterdam Avenue, New York, N.Y. 10027

Library of Congress Cataloging in Publication Data

Curtis, Sandra, R., 1950–
  The joy of movement in early childhood.

  (Early childhood education series)
  Bibliography: p.
  Includes index.
  1. Movement education. 2. Movement education—
Curricula. I. Title. II. Series.
GV452.C87   372.8 ´6   81-16520
                              AACR2

ISBN 0-8077-2692-3 (cloth)
ISBN 0-8077-2691-5 (paper)

Figure 65 has been copied from an illustration in M. V. Ridenour (ed.), *Motor Development: Issues and Applications* (Princeton, N.J.: Princeton Book Co., 1978), p. 220. Used by permission.

Manufactured in the United States of America

87 86 85 84 83 82   1 2 3 4 5 6

To my children, Danny and Debby,
who are the soul, spirit,
and joy of my life

Contents

Foreword   xi

Preface   xiii

1   Introduction   1

MOTOR DEVELOPMENT: A THEORETICAL BASE

2   Motor Development and Fundamental Motor
    Patterns   7
    PHYSICAL CHANGES 8
    FUNDAMENTAL MOTOR PATTERNS 9
    OBSERVATION HINTS 36

3   A Total Motor Activity Program   39
    MOTOR DEVELOPMENT 39
      Physical Components 39
      Environmental/Structural Components 41
      Instructional Components   41
    THE NATURE OF GAMES 46
    THE HOW TO'S 46

MOTOR ACTIVITIES:
A PRACTICAL GUIDE

4   Fundamental Movements   51

BODY PARTS AND BODY IMAGE ACTIVITIES   51
"Can You?" Challenges   51
Games for Body Parts and Body Image   51

FUNDAMENTAL MOTOR PATTERNS   61
Running   61
"Can You?" Challenges   61
Games for Running   62
Walking   65
"Can You?" Challenges   66
Games for Walking   66
Jumping   66
"Can You?" Challenges   67
Games for Jumping   67
Throwing and Catching   70
"Can You?" Challenges   70
Games for Throwing and Catching   71
Kicking   75
"Can You?" Challenges   75
Games for Kicking   76

5   Moving with Equipment   81

Balls   81
Ball Balancing Fun   81
Hoops and Tires   82
"Can You?" Challenges   82
Games   83
Ropes   85
"Can You?" Challenges   85
Group Activities   86
Bean Bags   87
"Can You?" Challenges   87
Games   87

Balance Beams and Boards   88
  "Can You?" Challenges on the Beam   88
  "Can You?" Challenges on the Balance Board   89
Mat Activities   89
  Stunts   89
  Group Activities   90
Obstacle Courses   95
Other Types of Equipment   96

6   Moving Without Equipment   **97**

  "Can You?" Challenges Stressing Movement Qualities   97
  More "Can You?" Challenges   98
  Group Activities   99
  Traditional Movement Songs   101

7   Health, Heart, and Safety   **103**

HEALTH AND THE HEART   103
HEALTH AND SAFETY   105

8   Playgrounds and Play Yards   **107**

CREATIVE PLAY SPACES   107
EQUIPMENT: MAKING AND BUYING   108

9   Sample Lessons   **117**

Appendix: Observation Checklists   **123**

Suggested References   **133**

Index   **135**

Foreword

About a half century ago Mary Gutteridge, in a study of motor development that was often quoted in child development textbooks, observed that four year olds were potentially capable of motor skills for which the nursery school environment of that time made little provision. Were she to repeat her study in today's early childhood centers, Dr. Gutteridge might well be impressed that some centers nowadays have more varied and challenging equipment. Whether she would find that young children generally are realizing their potential for movement is uncertain.

It would be unfair to say that movement has been neglected in the early childhood curriculum. Most programs provide equipment designed to enhance motor skills and offer children opportunities for participation in rhythms and dance. Only a few are so intent on preacademic skills as to relegate children's free movement to recess periods. On the other hand, one often looks in vain for evidence that teachers are as concerned with or as comfortable in assessing motor development and providing activities appropriate to the child's level of functioning as they are in dealing with other aspects of the child's development.

Textbooks dealing with child development and early education have not overlooked motor development, but the focus is more often on what the typical child of a given age can or cannot do than on the progression of events leading up to a particular skill. Early childhood education texts and books dealing more exclusively with movement for young children have been concerned with the integration of movement into the curriculum and with movement as a medium of expression. *The Joy of Movement* is quite compatible with these approaches but it offers something more, a finer-grained analysis of developing motor skills in the context of a wide variety of activities.

Recognizing that the teacher's capacity to provide for a particular child's motor activity is contingent on her ability to perceive accurately what the child is doing, Dr. Curtis shows the teacher what to look for. She then describes her view of a total motor activity program. Such a program, one notes, could be integrated into a variety of curriculum models. However, it is clear that Dr. Curtis's predilection is for a child-centered curriculum with a teacher who is both responsive and active.

The responsive teacher, sensitive not only to the children's levels of motor development, but also to their interests and social and emotional needs, will find appropriate ways to use and adapt the games that Dr. Curtis describes. Such games, growing out of and building on the spontaneous activities of the children, have an important place in any early childhood curriculum. One could imagine that they will be used with particularly good effect during the long days that are characteristic of day care.

Students contemplating their first ventures as teachers and teachers immersed in day-to-day responsibilities for a group of children will welcome the way Dr. Curtis has organized this book. The book's descriptions of specific activities, the sample lessons it offers, and the observation guide it provides all reveal an understanding of the many demands on teachers' time and the need for materials that are easy to use.

Although this book is clearly designed to show teachers how to promote the development of specific motor skills, its title *The Joy of Movement* suggests an outcome that goes well beyond any single skill. Children, it seems, always enjoy moving. The more skillful they are and the more coordinated and integrated their movements become, the more pleasure and self-satisfaction they derive from movement. And watching and supporting this process in children will surely bring joy in the children's movement to teachers themselves.

—Millie Almy, Professor of Education
University of California at Berkeley

Preface

This text was written for early childhood educators, day care providers, and other interested parents and professionals, to offer a framework for planning programs that will enhance motor development in young children. Recent research in the area of developmental movement has made it possible to focus movement programs that can specifically improve performance. This volume integrates the research to provide guidelines for observing children's movement, as well as specific program ideas. The first section discusses motor development from a theoretical base. The following section offers practical activities that can be used in program planning.

The value in a text such as this is that it can become a springboard for ideas from which individuals can then take off to create on their own. This book can be a starting place for exciting programs that will provide children with movement experiences that will reflect their own creativity, as well as the creativity of those who help them explore their movement potential. When both child and teacher are creatively exploring movement, then surely there will be real joy in movement.

I would like to thank Dr. Millie Almy for introducing me to this writing project. Through her generosity of time and guidance, I formulated many of the ideas in this book. She helped me formally define the interconnections between the disciplines of motor development and early childhood education. I would also like to extend special thanks to Lisa Haderlie Baker for her clear and complete illustrations and to Kay Fairwell, who patiently typed the manuscript. Finally, I would like to thank the children, staff, and parents of Beth El Nursery School and Jane

Gallagher's Day Care Home in Berkeley, California, for their help in playing the games, their suggestions and support, and the added bonus of the joy seen in the faces of the children in the photographs who verify the title of the book.

THE JOY
OF MOVEMENT
IN EARLY CHILDHOOD

Introduction

Movement is as natural and essential to young children's lives as loving care, rest, and nutrition. Movement provides children with an outlet for expression, creativity, and discovery. Through movement, children learn about themselves, their environment, and others. Movement is a stimulus for physical growth and development. The joy of movement is a child's expression of an emotional need fulfilled.

Young children are naturally busy, inquisitive movers. They learn by acting in their environment. Children enjoy moving for its own sake. The emotional satisfaction they receive from mastering physical skills is evident in the sheer determination they express preceding their triumphs and in the shining smiles that follow their accomplishments.

The images we share of young children involve a good deal of movement. Danny, three years old, challenges himself by building higher and higher towers to climb and jump from. Jennifer, at two and a half, splashes and kicks water in her pool, pretending she is swimming like her Daddy. Ben and Debbie, twenty-one and eighteen months, run up and down the block laughing for the sheer pleasure of running and because they are running together. Molly and Noah, both three, do not greet each other with words, but with lots of jumping, twirling, and spinning. Andrew, eighteen months, beams proudly after he arrives at the top of the climbing horse. Jamie, four, jumps endlessly off the bed for the freedom of the movement. Daniel, three and a half, jumps from his sandbox onto the knotted rope, swinging back and forth with his head arched back. The challenge, the success, the repetitions, and the joy shown in movement all are part of the moving world of young children.

Adults are just beginning to realize the benefits of movement for physical as well as mental health. One of our challenges as educators and care givers is to reinforce and enhance the movement capabilities of children. If the children with whom we work learn to cherish movement for its lifelong values, we will have contributed to their health and well-being.

The goal of this book is to provide teachers, parents, child care providers, and other interested persons with an effective way of facilitating the growth and development of motor skills in young children. There will obviously be many benefits. Children will learn, discover, and create in the process of developing their motor skills. The learning, discovering, and creating should not be minimized; they are bonuses derived from the primary concern of helping children use their bodies to enhance their own development.

The approach to movement expressed in this book is based on the following premises:

1. Enhancing the joy of movement early in life is a positive value for physical and mental health and development.
2. Children are active and use their bodies as tools of discovery.
3. Movement has value in and of itself. Its justification for value does not lie in what it can do to enhance academic learning. However, it is also valuable for expanding problem-solving abilities and enriching the learning experiences of children.
4. Adults and children facilitate motor development through creative structuring of the environment.
5. Exploration, problem solving, and feelings of success in response to a variety of challenges are the key to a successful motor development program for young children.

This book suggests ways to create a supportive environment in which children can experience a broad range of movement activities. The goal is not mastery of sports skills, but rather knowledge and control over how the body moves. This broad movement base may later be refined into sports skills as children grow. By allowing children the opportunity for success in movement activities, both individually and in groups, we can enhance their creativity and problem-solving skills, while specifically fostering physical development.

This book differs from other movement activity books for young children in several ways: in its philosophy of enhancing development, in its view of the roles of teachers and children, and in how to view a child's movement. The book's philosophy extends from children's innate drive for mastery over their environment: it encourages and takes advantage of the inquisitiveness, creativity, and problem-solving that are part of early childhood learning. The philosophy fits the nature of the child.

Teachers of movement are viewed as facilitators of children's learning. They work with children to explore, create challenges, and expand movement potential. They question, guide, discover, encourage, reinforce, and provide a helping hand. However, they do not teach in the traditional sense, nor do they merely supervise free play. They provide an environment in which learning can occur.

The focus on movement in this book is also different. Traditionally, the focus has been on the outcome of a movement, but here the focus is on what actually occurs during the movement. The teacher or parent is not encouraged to watch the outcome of a child's movement. Instead, the focus is on the process that occurs in order to produce the movement. Instead of how high Susie jumped, or how fast Jimmy ran, you will observe what the body was doing *during* the movement.

This approach requires the development of good observational skills and the use of some general background information concerning motor development and the acquisition of the basic fundamental movements. With a minimum of time and effort, you can learn to effectively plan programs to enhance motor development in young children.

MOTOR DEVELOPMENT: A THEORETICAL BASE

Motor Development and Fundamental Motor Patterns

Many developmental schedules are available that document the motoric capabilities of children at specific ages. While these schedules allow teachers to compare children with a norm, they generally are not very useful in helping adults know what to do with children to enhance their motor skills. The important thing to note when working with children on motor skills is that changes occur for all children, for some slowly, for others more quickly. For all children, these changes come through repetition, variation, and practice. There is an evolution of abilities that the child discovers as the abilities emerge. Exciting challenges, success, and lots of encouragement motivate children to practice and create more challenges. This in turn furthers the changes in a child's performance.

Motor development specialists have documented that all fundamental movement patterns emerge by age five. After this age, no new patterns develop; however, the process of refinement of these rudimentary skills takes ten to fifteen years. In the first year of life, children master one major obstacle—gravity. In addition, they develop increasing control of their hands. They learn to sit, stand, and move, as well as to manipulate objects. By the second year, walking is well under control; running, climbing, initial jumping, and rudimentary ball skills develop. Language and socialization help expand movement in the third year of life by providing concepts, labels, and playmates with which to explore. During the fourth and fifth years, more complex movement patterns occur, as well as rapid increases in speed and strength.

PHYSICAL CHANGES

One of the major factors in the development of motor skills during the first five years of life is physical growth. During the first year of life, children triple their weight, but their body proportions change very little. Head size remains about one-fourth of the total body length, compared with the adult head size which is about one-eighth of the body length. The four years following are characterized by major changes in body proportions: the arms and legs grow rapidly while the trunk grows somewhat more slowly. Height gains are twice that of weight gains during the second to the fifth year of life.

During these first five years, rapid bone growth accounts for much of the child's weight increase. Muscle tissue develops at a slower, more constant rate, equal to about one-fourth the weight gain per year. By age five, however, the muscle-tissue increase jumps to three-quarters of the weight gain. From ages three to six, strength increases by 65 percent. Increases in height add greater leverage to the limbs, which permits more speed in performing motor activities. After age five, the rapid increase in muscle tissue provides the strength and muscular energy necessary for expanding the child's skills.

Myelinization of the nervous system rapidly increases during these early years. Myelin is the sheathing that surrounds the nerve fibers. It increases conduction velocities of nerve impulses by insulating the fibers, resulting in more rapid initiation of movement responses and better coordination. Integration of reflexes through maturation of the nervous system inhibits specific movements and allows other movements to occur. The combination of physical growth factors, increased coordination, longer limbs for leverage, and strength development aids all children in naturally expanding their movement capabilities. The changes in physical growth explain much of the changes we see in movement over these first five years.

FUNDAMENTAL MOTOR PATTERNS

As the physical growth of children proceeds, a natural corresponding change occurs in movement patterns. Ralph Wickstrom did extensive research on the development of fundamental motor patterns.[1] He identifies these patterns as the basic language of movement. Just as notes are the basic language of music, and words are the basis of written language, so too is there a common basis for movement. In the same way that notes are developed into musical compositions and words into stories, fundamental movements develop into mature movement patterns, which form the basis for sports skills.

Among the fundamental motor patterns Wickstrom identifies are walking, running, jumping, kicking, throwing, and catching. These patterns emerge during the first five years of life. Wickstrom has identified developmental changes that occur as these patterns emerge. The patterns progress from an initial, minimal form to a mature form. The mature form establishes the base for the later sports skill form.

The changes that occur result from opportunities to practice movement in many situations and from physical growth. Changes occur in the timing and range of joint movements and in the speed with which body segments are integrated to work together to produce specific movements. The tables in this chapter show the development of fundamental motor patterns from their initial form to their mature form. Mature form is used in these charts as Wickstrom defined it, a pattern that "culminates early skill development and indicates readiness to progress to advanced sports skills."[2]

Many authors have attributed specific motor abilities to specific ages. However, ages are not used in the tables because the tables are intended to help you establish what level children have reached in terms of the development of patterns, and to learn how these patterns progress. It is important to reemphasize that performance changes come with opportunities to practice

---

[1] *Fundamental Motor Patterns*, 2nd ed. (Philadelphia: Lea & Febiger, 1977).
[2] *Fundamental Motor Patterns*, p. 11.

and physical maturation. All children progress at different rates. Children should be evaluated in terms of their functioning as individuals, and programs should be planned from that point, rather than from a comparison to age-ability norms.

Throughout the text, differences in performance between boys and girls are noted. While girls often perform better than boys on balance and body control tasks, boys generally perform better on skills like throwing and jumping. Research on sex differences in motor performance in early childhood is beginning to interest many individuals. The next few years will add new and interesting information to our limited knowledge base in this area.

CHILDREN WITH SPECIAL NEEDS

This book does not deal specifically with children who have disabling conditions, whether they be sensory, emotional, learning, or physical. Many of these children are being mainstreamed into early childhood programs, and teachers must deal with their discomfort and lack of knowledge of how to interact with children with special needs. It is important for early childhood educators to recognize that these children are much more similar to nondisabled children than they are different. For most even their movement patterns proceed in the same developmental manner, though some children progress much more slowly in their acquisition of motor skills. It generally takes children with disabilities longer to progress from the initial to the mature form of a fundamental motor pattern, and some may never reach the mature form. The most effective way to improve the motor skills of young children with disabilities is exactly the same as with nondisabled children. Although they may need equipment adaptations, what they need most is to be challenged, encouraged to try, reinforced for their successes, and involved in the decision-making processes. They too will improve upon their initial levels.

Walking

Walking marks the emergence of children from infancy into the toddler phase. It is a child's most remarkable motoric accomplishment. Every proud parent attests to the importance of achieving upright locomotion by his or her enthusiastic encouragement: "Come on, that's a girl, come to Mommy!" The initial robot-like walking movements of the toddler gradually progress to a fluid walking pattern after hours of practice and corresponding physical maturation. (See Table 1.)

In general, the immature walking pattern (see Figure 1) is useful for stability—the wide base and choppy exaggerated steps with the arms up in the high-guard position help protect children as they learn to cope with the demands of upright locomotion. Also, walking and running are cyclical—the right and left sides of the body repeat the cycle of movements. Discrepancies between the two sides of the body should be noted. Most children demonstrate the basic mature walking pattern by age two (see Figure 2). Between ages two and three, coordination and rhythm of the arms and legs improve. By age five, differences between children and adults are indistinguishable by mere observation.

Table 1   Walking

Initial	Mature
Short steps.	Increased step length.
Flat-foot contact, knee bent as foot touches ground, then quick knee straightening. Relatively no ankle movement. Leg bent excessively.	Heel contacts ground with the knee straight; weight rolls forward so toe pushes; then knee bends as it is lifted off the ground.
Toes point out.	Toes generally point straight ahead.
Feet spread apart wide.	Feet are placed closer together, narrowing the base of support.
Slight forward lean.	Forward lean decreases.
No hip rotation.	Hip rotates back to the support leg, then forward to the side of the moving leg.
Arms held up with elbows bent for protection against falls (high-guard position).	Arms held straight, swing easily at sides of body.

Source: Tables 1–7 have been adapted from Ralph Wickstrom, *Fundamental Motor Patterns*, 2nd ed. (Philadelphia: Lea & Febiger, 1977).

Running

Running naturally flows from walking. Children's first attempts at a run are rapid walking steps. Young runners seem to move their legs directly under their bodies in stiff, choppy steps, as though to prevent an almost inevitable tumble.

Running itself is characterized by a period of nonsupport when the body is airborne. Beginning walkers may try to walk quickly when encouraged to "run to Daddy." In general, however, they are not able to propel their bodies into the air until about eighteen months of age. The strength, balance, and coordination necessary to perform the minimum requirements of running gradually develop by age two. By age five, children usually exhibit the basic mature form of running. Refinement of the

Figure 1 Walking pattern of a fourteen month old. He uses short steps as he puts his feet down flat. His toes are pointed out and his feet are spread apart. He keeps his arms in the high-guard position for protection in case he falls.

Figure 2   Mature walking pattern of a three year old. The right and left sides of the body repeat the cycle of movement.

mature pattern continues through puberty, and this refinement is reflected in increasing speed. (See Table 2.) The children pictured in Figures 3–6 show different levels of running patterns and some of the problems encountered when learning to run.

Jumping

Jumping is defined as propelling the body off the ground with one or two feet. Hopping is a variation on jumping that develops as the nervous system matures. In hopping, children take off on one foot and land on the same foot. Leaping is another variation where children take off on one foot and land on the oppo- site foot.

Jumping begins soon after children begin to walk comfor- tably and consistently. Generally, from eighteen to twenty-four months, children become prolific jumpers, often to the chagrin of their care givers. Children climb up and jump down from such things as stairs, curbs, ledges, and benches. A definite develop-

Table 2 Running

Initial	Mature
Arms held straight, very little movement—mainly to help maintain balance.	Arms bent and swung in a diagonal pattern in opposition to the leg action—that is, right arm forward when left leg is forward. Elbow brought up parallel with shoulder.
Short stride.	Increase in stride length.
Slow running speed.	Increase in running speed.
Support leg (back leg) straightens slowly as child takes off.	Support leg pushes off forcefully by straightening behind the buttocks.
No trunk lean.	Slight forward trunk lean.
Leg is bent at a low level as it comes forward. Motion of knee is out to the side and then forward.	Knee lifted high as leg comes forward, and the heel of the foot is brought close to the buttocks.
Toes point out.	Toes point forward.

mental sequence is evident in jumping ability. The progressive order of difficulty in jumping is presented in the following sequence.

1. Stepping down from one foot to the other foot (generally off a step)
2. Stepping down from one foot to two feet
3. Stepping down from two feet to two feet (See Figure 7.)
4. Running and jumping forward from one foot to the other foot
5. Jumping forward from two feet to two feet (standing broad jump)
6. Running and jumping forward from one foot to two feet
7. Jumping over an object from two feet to two feet
8. Rhythmic hopping—one foot to the same foot (Girls are generally better at hopping due to their advanced maturational levels.)

Figure 3   A two year old with a fairly mature running pattern. She has many elements of a mature pattern: a long stride in which she pushes off the balls of her feet, toes pointed forward, and knees lifted straight. However, she uses little arm action and has no forward trunk lean.

Figure 4   A three year old with some restricted arm action, short stride length, and a flat-footed push-off, but with good knee action and forward trunk lean.

Figure 5 Another three year old with effective arm action, but low knee and heel movement, a flat-footed takeoff, and toes that point out. He has some forward trunk lean and good stride length.

Figure 6   A four year old who has all the basics for a mature running pattern. Notice the diagonal arm action across the chest, the high knee and heel lift, the push off the balls of her feet, and also the forward trunk lean.

The height of the jump, be it down from something, or up over something, seriously affects the form children will use to master the task. As the height increases, children will very likely revert to previous developmental levels in order to perform the task. By age three children can generally jump down from about two feet, jump forward one to three feet, and jump up and over something one to two feet high.

Two types of jumps will be discussed in terms of initial and mature form—the standing long jump and the vertical jump.

STANDING LONG JUMP
The child tries to jump as far forward as possible from a two-foot takeoff to a two-foot landing. (See Table 3.) Figures 8 and 9 illustrate initial and more mature standing long jump patterns.

(continued on page 20)

Figure 7   Free-spirited, two-footed jump from a bench by a three year old.

Table 3   Standing Long Jump

Initial	Mature
Arms move to back and up as body moves forward.	Body gets positioned for the jump by crouching and swinging the arms up and back.
Arms stay up at sides in high-guard position for balance.	Arms are swung forcefully forward and up as the body straightens at the hips and ankles to lift off the ground.
One-foot takeoff.	Two-foot takeoff.
Body does not straighten fully while in the air.	Body fully extended in air.
Hips and knees begin to bend in preparation for the landing while airborne.	Once in the air, the knee bends as do the hips. Knees straighten and reach the ground, arms come forward and down.
Stepping or one-foot landing.	Two-foot landing.

Figure 8   Standing long jump of a three year old. Notice the minimal crouch, how the arms are not fully extended back, how the body is only lifted a little into the air, and the stepping landing.

Figure 9   A four year old performs a standing long jump. He uses an effective crouch but does not extend his arms back at all. He does get some body extension in the air and prepares for a two-footed landing.

VERTICAL JUMP

The child jumps straight up, generally in an attempt to reach an object. (See Table 4.) Figures 10–12 show the progression from an initial to a mature vertical jumping pattern.

Table 4   Vertical Jump

Initial	Mature
Very minimal crouch.	Knees, hips, and ankles bend in crouch in preparation of jumping.
Arms are raised to side as jump starts. Arms may swing out to back if not given target to reach for.	Arms forcefully lift body.
Hips and knees bend in air on takeoff.	Hips, knees, and ankles straighten forcefully as body goes up.
Slight forward lean during push-off.	Body remains straight until landing, then hips, knees, and ankles bend to absorb the shock.
Stepping or one-foot landing.	Two-foot landing.

Figure 10   An initial vertical jumping pattern of a three year old. He uses a minimal crouch and very little force with his arms as they are raised, and his knees are bent in the air. He does take off and land on two feet.

Figure 11   This four year old crouches too deeply for an effective jump. He uses his arms forcefully to lift his body, straightens his body while in the air, and takes off and lands on two feet.

Figure 12   This four year old demonstrates an effective initial crouch and forceful arm action. His body straightens in the air, and he takes off and lands on both feet. He shows a mature vertical jumping pattern.

Observation of children's vertical jumps shows that arm action differs greatly between jumps with and without targets. Try observing several children in both situations to see how their jumps differ. Children may throw their arms out behind them, rather than up if they have no target. This action is called "winging out" and impedes upward movement. Therefore, be sure to provide a target for the children to jump towards.

Throwing

Children begin throwing early in the first year as they practice grasping and releasing objects. There are four stages in throwing that show the progression to the mature pattern. (See Table 5 and Figures 13–17.)

Our culture has emphasized throwing activities for boys more than for girls and while there is great variability among children,

(continued on page 26)

Figure 13 A fifteen month old showing a Stage 1 throwing pattern. The ball is held near the ear and then pushed forward and down.

Figure 14 A two-year-old girl shows a Stage 2 throwing motion. She has some body rotation, her hand is cocked behind her head, and she uses no foot movement.

Table 5   Throwing

Stage 1	Stage 2
1. Feet are stationary. 2. Ball is held near ear. Child pushes ball straight down. 3. No rotation of body or step forward.	1. Some body rotation to side opposite throwing arm. 2. Hand holds ball cocked behind the head. 3. No foot movement.
Stage 3	**Stage 4: Step–Turn–Throw**
1. Arm and trunk movements are the same as in Stage 2. 2. Child steps forward on foot that is on *same* side of body as throwing arm.	1. As movement is begun, body weight shifts to side with ball 2. Arm is brought up and back behind head. 3. Weight is transferred by a step to foot that is on the *opposite* side of body as throwing arm. 4. Trunk rotates to opposite side. 5. Ball is released as elbow is straightened with a whipping motion.

Figure 15   Example of a Stage 2 throwing pattern in a four-year-old girl showing no foot movement, hand cocked near her head, and some body rotation.

Figure 16   These photographs show a three-year-old boy with a Stage 3 throwing pattern. Notice how he steps forward on the foot that is on the same side as his throwing arm.

Figure 17   A three year old demonstrates a Stage 4 throwing pattern. He shifts his weight to the side with the ball, his trunk rotates with the throw, and he transfers his weight to the opposite foot as the ball is released with a whipping motion of his arm and wrist.

marked sex differences in throwing ability are evident by five years of age. There are no known physical reasons for girls to be poorer at throwing than boys at this early age, but the lack of practice and encouragement for girls clearly reinforces our cultural stereotypes. The differences in the maturity pattern of boys and girls of the same age are clearly evident in the two three year olds shown in Figures 15 and 18.

Throwing patterns are very interesting to observe. Due to cultural influences, many girls and women never move further along in the developmental sequence than Stage 3. Ask some of the female teachers or parents to throw a ball as confirmation of this observation. It is rare for men to show the same Stage 3 movement pattern. If young girls receive the same opportunities and encouragement as young boys to participate in throwing activities, over time there may be a definite impact on sex differences in throwing performance.

Catching

Catching is perhaps the most difficult skill for children to master. There are a number of variables that affect catching. Some of these variables include the size of the ball (larger balls are easier), the path of the ball through the air (low is easier), the distance between the thrower and catcher (closer is easier), the speed with

Figure 18   A four year old demonstrates his Stage 4 throwing pattern, basically a step-turn-throw motion.

which the ball is thrown, whether the child must move to catch the ball, and, if so, in what direction.

The perceptual requirements for catching are quite complex. A child must, from the moment the ball is released, be able to judge where it will land and how soon it will get to a particular spot. These perceptual skills do not develop until children are in the upper elementary grades. Consequently, preschoolers are perceptually just not ready to shag fly balls hit to the outfield.

As with throwing, there are progressive stages that lead to the development of mature catching. (See Table 6.) Mature catching is basically a matter of using the body to absorb the force of the ball. Various stages in the development of catching skills are shown in Figures 19–21.

Table 6   Catching

Stage 1	Stage 2
1. Arms are held out straight in front of the body, with palms up. 2. When ball makes contact with arms, elbows bend. Child tries to trap ball against chest. May clap at ball or use hands like a vise if ball is small. 3. May turn head to side and lean back.	1. Arms are in front, with elbows slightly bent. 2. As ball approaches, arms encircle it at chest. 3. Robotlike performance.
Stage 3	**Stage 4**
1. Arms are bent. 2. Ball bounces on chest, then is controlled with arms. 3. Tries to catch with hands but may resort to using chest.	1. Hands are positioned to intercept ball. 2. Grasps and controls ball. 3. Gives way to force of ball by bending at hips and knees. 4. Absorbs force by continuing to move and give way in direction ball came from.

Figure 19 A four-year-old girl tries to catch the ball. Her arms are slightly bent, she does not move toward the ball, nor does she attempt to trap it. She shows the basic characteristics of the Stage 1 development in catching.

Figure 20 This series of photographs shows a four-year-old boy at a Stage 1 level of catching development. Initially he uses his hands like a vise as he watches the ball. As it approaches, he spreads his arms, tries to trap the ball on his chest, turns his head away, and drops the ball.

Kicking

Kicking is a pattern that develops soon after children begin to run. Young toddlers can often be seen nudging a ball forward along the ground, making contact with it against the front of the lower leg. As the kicking pattern develops, children develop better balance which they use to get greater force and leverage on the leg swing that contacts the ball. Stages that have been identified in kicking patterns are shown in Table 7. In general, the changes that occur in kicking are from a fairly straight pendular motion

Figure 21   This four year old shows characteristics of both Stage 3 and Stage 4 in his catching pattern. Although he turns his head when he clasps the ball, he does position his hands correctly for catching. He is successful at grasping and controlling the ball with his hands, and he absorbs the force of the ball by bending his hips and knees.

Table 7   Kicking

Stage 1	Stage 2
1. Kicking leg is straight, moved up, and forward. 2. No accompanying body movement.	1. Lower part of kicking leg is lifted up and behind body to prepare for kick.

Stage 3	Stage 4
1. Upper leg is brought back, with knee bent. 2. Leg swings through greater arc than in Stage 2. 3. Some body adjustments. 4. Leg may be overcocked resulting in loss of mechanical advantage.	1. Hip and knee are cocked effectively. 2. Trunk leans backward. 3. Leg moves through greater range of motion. 4. Knee straightens as leg swings through to contact ball. 5. Arm and body adjustments are made during follow-through. 6. Starts farther behind ball and moves total body into it.

of the leg with little body movement to a whipping leg motion that involves the entire body.

It is interesting to note that young children often pull back their kicking leg once they have kicked the ball, not allowing the momentum of their leg to carry their body forward on the follow-through. As children mature, they learn to kick *through* the ball rather than *at* the ball, as they do initially. Figures 22–25 illustrate this developmental pattern. One way to encourage follow-through is to suggest that the child approach the ball with quick steps forward.

Climbing

Climbing is an important total body movement pattern that matures over time. The contribution of climbing to general motor development has been well documented. The climbing progression generally begins as children creep up stairs, because the movement pattern of creeping on hands and knees is the same whether going along the floor or up stairs. Children begin to

Figure 22   A two year old demonstrating a Stage 1 kicking pattern. Her kicking leg is straight and she has no other body movement.

Figure 23   This five year old has some of the characteristics of a Stage 2 kicking pattern. She brings her kicking leg up behind her to prepare for the kick. She shows some accompanying body movement in her left arm, indicating transition to Stage 3.

Figure 24   This series of photographs shows a four year old who pulls back his leg once he kicks the ball. Typical of children at this stage of kicking development, he does not allow the momentum of his leg to carry him forward on his follow-through. He kicks at the ball rather than through the ball. Although he does start behind the ball and moves into it as he kicks it, his developmental pattern is characteristic of a basic Stage 3 kicking pattern. He makes some body adjustments and uses a small arc for his leg swing.

Figure 25 This four year old effectively kicks through the ball demonstrating a Stage 4 kicking pattern. He starts behind the ball, moves into it, cocks his knee and hip, leans his trunk back, straightens his knee as he contacts the ball, and then adjusts his body on the follow-through.

climb stairs soon after they start to walk. They grab the nearest hand or handrail for support. The familiar pattern of "marking time" is evident as children progress in stair climbing ability: The child puts one foot up the step, then brings the other foot to the same step as if marching in place, and finally follows up by bringing the lead foot to the next step. (See Figure 26.) Gradually, children learn to go up steps in an alternating foot pattern.

Figure 26 A two year old "marks time" as she ascends the steps.

Children learn to climb stairs before they can successfully come down. Very often, young children will creep or walk up a flight of stairs, only to wail as they reach the top because they can't come down. The initial method children use to descend stairs is to creep down, feet first. Some children go down head first, controlling their downward slide with their arms.

The main problem associated with stair climbing relates to the height of the steps themselves. Shorter steps encourage earlier climbing and are less of a hazard if the child falls. The ability to climb stairs depends enormously on the opportunity to practice.

Ladder climbing presents problems similar to stair climbing. The distance between the rungs of a ladder may encourage or discourage exploration. Rungs that are a short distance apart are the best. In addition, the steeper the incline of the ladder, the more difficult the task. Children "mark time" on ladders just as they do on steps: they take the lead foot up and bring the trailing foot to the same rung. They then lead again with the initial foot.

Children climb on rocks, fences, trees, playhouses, and all sorts of contraptions. Hand placement is particularly important as children learn to climb. Knowing how to transfer hand positions can make most children successful and safe climbers. Figure 27 illustrates good climbing form. In general, hands should be in front, rather than behind the body. Children should be encouraged to put their thumbs around the bar they are holding. They should also learn to turn so that their bodies face the object they are climbing over, rather than to position their hands behind themselves and then climb with their back facing the object. Preferably, only one body part should be moved at a time, leaving the others in place for support.

Balance

Balance is often dealt with as a separate category of motor performance. It is one of the most fundamental components of movement activities. Balancing ability is very specific to different movements. For example, maintaining balance while crossing a balance beam is different from balancing on one leg while kicking a ball. The balance required in skiing is quite different from the

Figure 27   This girl demonstrates good climbing form: body faces the jungle gym, thumbs are around the bars, and one body part is moving at a time. She descends in the same way.

ability to stay upright on a tilting board. If children are given a variety of movement experiences and an opportunity to practice in a motivating, challenging environment, they will improve their balancing abilities in very creative ways.

In general, balance ability improves as children learn to use internal and external cues to help them remain upright. The internal cues come from muscles and joints. The external cues are primarily visual. It is easy to explain internal cues. If you stand on one leg with your eyes closed, you will notice that you can balance, but there is a good deal of rocking, swaying, and excess movement. If you then open your eyes, most of the extra movement will stop. While you could maintain balance quite adequately using only internal cues, it is more difficult than with visual cues. With practice, you could noticeably improve your balance with eyes closed, but most people look at one object in the environment while balancing. This object provides a stable external cue. If, however, you move your eyes in any random fashion, you will again notice more swaying and less-stable balance.

This information can be useful in helping children develop good balancing skills through an awareness of how they use internal and external cues. There are seven general concepts about balance that will help to facilitate balance development. These can also serve as "Can You?" challenges for your children.

1. Balance is easier on a large base than on a small base.
2. Balance is harder on a moving than on a stationary base.
3. Keeping the body weight over the base of support makes balance easier.
4. Moving various body parts to different positions can make balance easier or harder.
5. Using a visual focal point makes balancing easier.
6. Lowering the body weight (or center of gravity) makes balancing easier.
7. Smooth surfaces are harder to balance on than textured surfaces.

OBSERVATION HINTS

1. View the child's movement from several angles: in front, from behind, and to the side. Children look different in their performance when viewed from different angles. Sometimes you may be able to spot a movement problem by looking at the child from a different angle. Often when we observe children face to face, our observations are severely limited. For instance, if you were observing children running toward you, you might not see, as a side view might show, that their feet were contacting the ground flat-footed rather than in a heel-toe fashion.

2. Make comparisons between children playing together. One of the best means of observing performance is watching children who are doing the same activities. It is easy to note which child is crouching too far down to jump effectively when you can compare that child with a child who uses an effective crouch.

3. View children from several different age groups. Children of the same age perform very differently, yet all may be performing within the normal developmental range. A two, three, and four year old all may be Stage 2 throwers, and yet another group

of children of the same age may be Stage 3 throwers. Variability is part of the development of motor performance, and the best way to obtain perspective on this is to view many children at several ages doing the same activity.

4. Look at the major joints of the body (hips, knees, ankles, shoulders, elbows) to see what is happening during each movement. Begin by looking at leg action, then watch arm action, and finally try to view the whole movement. The most common way to observe motor performance is to watch where the ball went, or how high the jump was. This is called the *outcome* of the movement. If you focus on movement outcomes, you do not get any information on what the body was doing to produce that movement, and consequently, you cannot suggest ways to improve the performance. If children are jumping to reach balloons suspended from strings and are not successful, you may note that they were crouching too deeply to start. By focusing on the body rather than on the outcome, you can make useful suggestions on how to begin on the next try. You may even have another child demonstrate a successful starting position.

3

A Total Motor Activity Program

MOTOR DEVELOPMENT

Growth and maturation are necessary for many of the changes that occur in motor development during the preschool years. However, good physical activity programs enhance development by providing challenging activities that fit into a total framework of motor development. There are three essential components in a motor development framework. These include: (1) the physical components of movement, (2) the environmental/structural components, and (3) the instructional components.

Physical Components

1. Physical fitness
   a. Muscle strength: the amount of force that a particular muscle group can exert in a specific movement (e.g., the total weight one arm can lift)
   b. Muscular endurance: the ability of specific muscle groups to exert force over a long period of time (e.g., the number of situps completed in one minute)
   c. Cardiovascular endurance: the ability of the heart and lungs to transfer oxygen to the working muscles (e.g., running continuously for fifteen minutes)
   d. Flexibility: the range of motion of the joints (e.g., leaning forward to touch your toes without bending the knees)

2. Neuromotor: the integration of the nervous and muscular systems
    a. Reaction time: how fast a movement is completed in reaction to a stimulus (e.g., jumping and touching the target as soon as you hear the bell)
    b. Coordination: integrating specific muscle actions into efficient movement skills (e.g., combining a step with a hop and alternating your feet to get a skipping movement)
    c. Speed: how fast a particular movement can be accomplished (e.g., running one hundred yards in fifteen seconds)
    d. Agility: the ability to quickly change movement patterns as stimuli change (e.g., dodging a ball as it comes toward you)
3. Perceptual/motor: the integration of information from the sensory receptors with the muscle response
    a. Posture and balance: maintaining the body in an upright position, centered over the base of support (e.g., standing on one foot with eyes closed)
    b. Body image: how an individual views his or her own body (e.g., drawing a picture of your body)
    c. Form perception: recognizing shapes in space (e.g., distinguishing between the letters *b* and *d*)
    d. Spatial orientation: orienting the body in space (e.g., lining up with your back next to the wall)
    e. Laterality: knowing right and left (e.g., following directions to pick up a bean bag in your right hand and drop it to your right foot)
    f. Directionality: knowing directions like up, down, forward, back, under and over (e.g., following instructions to climb over a bar and then go under it)
    g. Figure-ground discrimination: distinguishing the background from the foreground (e.g., following directions to run to the nearest basketball hoop on the playground)
    h. Kinesthesis: having information on the body's position in space derived from the muscles and joints without the aid of vision (e.g., with your eyes closed, touching your nose)
    i. Eye-hand coordination: using eyes and hands together to accomplish a task (e.g., bouncing a ball five times)

   j. Eye-foot coordination: using eyes and feet together to accomplish a task (e.g., kicking a ball along the line)
   k. Sequencing: combining movement patterns (e.g., doing three jumps in place, then bouncing the ball and catching it)
   l. Auditory discrimination: distinguishing auditory cues (e.g., starting to run on one whistle and stopping on two)
4. Movement patterns
   a. Locomotor patterns: walk, run, jump, skip, gallop, hop
   b. Non-locomotor patterns: bend, stretch, push, pull, swing, sway, twist, turn, curl, fall, stand, sit, kneel, reach
5. Quality of movement: use of time, space, and force
   a. Time: slow, medium, fast
   b. Space: low, medium, high; horizontal, vertical, diagonal
   c. Force: light, medium, heavy

Environmental/Structural Components

Movement occurs either in an environment that is open or in one that is structured in some manner by equipment. Moving through an environment becomes unique by virtue of the way in which the environmental space is used. Adults along with children can plan environments for movement that provide an endless variety of challenges and discoveries. The variables to be manipulated include:

1. Group size: small groups, individuals, teams, partners, all girls, all tall children, and so forth
2. Equipment: the number of pieces and types of equipment to be used—one ball or rope for each child, one per team, one per class; small ball, light balls; and so forth
3. Boundaries: large volleyball court, hopscotch area, dodgeball circles, and so forth
4. Time: short activities that change every five minutes, one activity lasting the whole period, and so forth

Instructional Components

From the beginning this book has stressed making movement creative, challenging, and motivating for children. A special dynamic relationship binds the adult and child involved in this type of motor activity. When children are made a part of the decision-making process, they know that the adult approves of their ideas. They then have a stake in making the ideas succeed, while they also have their self-concept bolstered. This is very important. Behavior problems often disappear when children are creatively working on their *own* activities.

In addition, educators of young children try to emphasize the development of problem-solving skills. These skills can be applied to all aspects of the child's study, including movement, math, reading, and science. Kamii and DeVries' *Group Games in Early Education*[1] suggests that games are an important way for children to develop autonomy and problem-solving ability, while becoming less egocentric. Given the opportunity to learn new games, children also learn new ways of cooperating with others in a group. In good games, children are challenged and interested. They can judge their own success while actively participating physically and/or mentally.

Kamii and DeVries' view regarding the teacher's role is consistent with that expressed in this book. The teacher's role is to facilitate children's interaction, but not to dominate it. Knowing when and how to step in and out are critical judgments for the teacher. The teacher must be ready to help children over an impasse, yet also be ready to step aside so that they do not rely on the teacher for solutions to problems they can solve themselves.

Some teachers are naturally effective at this type of interaction with children. Others let children do what they can with movement, while they themselves interact primarily to maintain a safe environment. Most teachers are creative about varying the child's environment, but lack a specific focus for improving children's movement abilities through changes in the environment, or for evaluating improvement. It is possible to learn to be effective at guiding children in problem-solving for movement activities.

It can be extremely frustrating for anyone to be given a problem without sufficient tools (methods, techniques, or knowledge)

---

[1]C. Kamii and R. DeVries, *Group Games in Early Education: Implications of Piaget's Theory* (Washington, D.C.: National Association for the Education of Young Children, 1980).

to solve it. Mouska Mosston has presented a clear and concise teaching method called Command to Discovery teaching, which stresses creative problem-solving in physical activities.[2] Mosston has much to offer early childhood educators, because he focuses on individualization of instruction and enhancing cognitive processing. He utilizes a process of shifting decision-making from the adults to the children.

In order to shift this process from the adult to the child, Mosston presents a progression of teaching styles. The progression is as follows:

1. Command: The teacher directs the entire activity and controls all the variables.
2. Task: The teacher explains a task and the students do it in their own time.
3. Reciprocal teaching: Children are paired and work together to develop skills. They correct each other's errors.
4. Small groups: This is an extended reciprocal style with three or four children in which some do the skill, others observe, others record.
5. Individual program: The teacher designs individual programs. Students follow through on their own.
6. Guided discovery: Students are challenged to come up with solutions to group or individual movement problems. The teacher asks questions that guide students to a correct response but does *not* give the answers. The teacher typically asks a "How can you . . . ?" question and then helps suggest alternative solutions like "What would happen if you . . . ?" eventually leading to group discovery by consensus.
7. Problem-solving: The students are expected to seek out solutions completely on their own.

There are elements of Mosston's various styles in all teaching. The most common, however, are the command style and the individual program. Rarely are children encouraged to solve problems in a group or with a partner. Still more rare is the guided discovery approach, which has the greatest value to cognitive

---

[2]*Teaching Physical Education: From Command to Discovery* (Columbus, Ohio: Charles Merrill Publishing Company, 1966).

development by helping children develop problem solving skills.

Certainly preschoolers cannot be expected to solve very complex movement problems. However, they can be encouraged over time to seek solutions to simple problems and to be involved in the decision-making processes. When Mosston's approach is combined with a movement education approach, the basis for thinking, questioning, and challenging becomes a natural part of the process itself.

Movement education is by now quite familiar to many movement specialists. It was developed in England after World War II and extended to Western Europe. The aim of movement education is to provide children with a broad and comprehensive basis of movement experiences so they can develop their own movement resources to the fullest potential. It has come to the United States and developed into a method of exploring movement through "Can you . . . ?" type challenges for children, such as, "Can you jump over the rope?" "Can you slide under the rope?" "Can you roll the ball along the rope?" Traditionally the challenges have come from the teacher. By combining some of Mosston's teaching ideas with the movement education approach, a dynamic physical activity program emerges which can be called *movement exploration.*

An illustration of this combined approach of movement exploration is the game Balloon Jumpers described on page 67. Once the children have tried to jump and reach the balloons, they may find the task too hard or too easy. "How can we change the balloons to make it easier?" you may ask. Depending on the responses, you can adjust the balloons. This process may be repeated several times regarding the height of the balloons. Or, you may change the question and ask the children to vary how they get up to the balloons, such as jumping or leaping to them. In another example, you may use two pieces of equipment like a tire and a rope stretched out to begin an obstacle course. Have the children jump into the hoop and walk along the rope. Then suggest that the children get two more pieces of equipment to add to the obstacle course. They can then decide what movements to do on the new equipment. You can have the children decide to change how they move on the equipment. Instead of jumping in the hoop they may walk around the edge and jump over the rope. Another approach is to ask children to get equipment to jump over and arrange an obstacle course specifically for jumping. Decisions like these help children create an exciting movement environment to play and grow in.

A personal reminder: as the initiator of the movement program, you must find a style of teaching that is comfortable for you. It will naturally take time to develop a feel for what is expected from the various teaching styles and how they relate to movement. For example, anticipating expected movement problems is necessary to make the guided discovery approach a success. Only a person who has experimented with various movements and has observed many children will become proficient at this approach. Yet this approach is critical to helping children learn to become effective problem solvers. In a way, using the approach well is the adult problem-solving end of the experience.

Remember that when you are experimenting with various styles, children should always be permitted to make some of their own decisions. At first the decisions may be limited to where to play the activity or how many times to jump over the rope. Gradually shift more challenging decisions to them.

The beauty of the movement approach is that it is by trial and error, constantly changing, like the children and life itself. You will at times feel frustrated that the children did not get what you wanted them to get out of the activity. Often young children need a week of exposure to a new activity before they really understand it. They may not learn the game right away but they are in the process of learning. The children's level of understanding may be simply learned ritual or repetitive play, or they may understand some but not all the rules. Be patient in your expectations of movement outcomes. The value in a lesson may be very different than you had planned. You may need to rethink how you can try for the movement experience you were aiming at, or you may decide to abandon that particular goal because you have discovered a new, more important one.

THE NATURE OF GAMES

Children can learn to cooperate and to be competitive. Both types of behavior have a place in our society. Most game and sport activities are competitive, yet there is a great amount of cooperative behavior that must be achieved in order for teams to be successful. Competition in and of itself is not harmful. If winning and losing are handled casually, if boastfulness is discouraged, and if children are given the choice of whether or not to compete, there should be little problem with including competitive games as part of the movement program. The section "Motor Activities: A Practical Guide" includes both cooperative games, in which children work together for common goals, and competitive games.

THE HOW TO'S

Here you are, faced with a bright-eyed, cheery group of wiggling, fidgety youngsters. How do you decide what to do, how to do it, and what should happen? How do you begin to know what they need in terms of movement experiences? Start to evaluate their needs with a few simple challenges focusing on the level of their fundamental motor patterns.

> Who can walk across the room?
> Who can run back and sit down?
> Who can jump?

Jot down general notes about what you see. Use the observation checklists in the back of this book. It is not necessary, however, to spend a lot of time assessing the children's exact levels. Get a general idea and then plunge into your program. Assessment should be an ongoing part of your program through the observations you make on daily occurrences.

Decide on a movement theme for the activity period. It may be jumping, exploring balance, being airborne, moving like animals, stopping and starting, or falling. Let the children guide the pace of the activity and the time to interject new challenges or change groups. Start the activity session with slow movements, build up to more vigorous activity, then taper down to slow activities. Get your feet wet—begin. Remember to encourage the children, smile, and be positive about their skills.

MOTOR ACTIVITIES: A PRACTICAL GUIDE

All the activities in this section are considered skeletons or frames. The imagination and creativity you and the children bring to these activities will fill them out and create special movement experiences. The variations at the end of each activity can be used to change one of the motor activity components (physical, environmental, or instructional).

Through the year, the children will become more and more adept at the games and activities included in this section. Their growing cognitive abilities and improved motor skills will permit a greater range of movement possibilities. They will understand how to create new movement challenges and how to change games in exciting ways. The initial stumbling blocks, like keeping track of points, should be eliminated initially and added as the children learn the games. As the children gain a sense of autonomy and understanding of the game rules, they will play the game with increased confidence. Generally, if children are interested and excited about an activity, they will want to play it again and again. If not, take your cues from the children and begin something different. You can reintroduce the activity at another time, in another way, or in another group.

4

Fundamental Movements

BODY PARTS AND BODY IMAGE ACTIVITIES

"CAN YOU?" CHALLENGES

Other skill development: flexibility, balance, laterality
Call out various body parts and have the children touch these parts on themselves or use them in some manner: touch your eyes, nose, toes; rub your elbows; touch right elbow to left knee, right foot to right ear.
Variations:

1. Have different children take turns being the caller for the entire group.
2. Have the children explore some "cannots" like: touch your elbows together behind your back. Help the children develop a list of these.
3. Break into small groups and have children rotate being the caller.
4. Have children pair up and challenge one another. They can either demonstrate or verbally describe the challenge.
5. Add fast/slow components, for example, clap your right knee with your left hand three times very fast.
6. Identify body parts on partners. Emphasize where right and left are on another child.
7. Use bean bags to balance on top of various body parts.

GAMES FOR BODY PARTS AND BODY IMAGE

Points
Other skill development: balance, flexibility
In this game, each body part that can support body weight counts as one point. (See Figure 28.) Points include hands, fingers, the

Figure 28 The game of Points.

buttocks, knees, elbows, heels, and feet. To introduce the game, have the children try to balance on two specific points with you. Then have them try their own ideas. Call attention to interesting combinations you see the children doing. Ask the children to identify the body parts they are on. Have them try other two-point balancing, then one-point and three-point balancing.

Once the children understand the game, vary the format in any of these ways:

1. Change the groupings to increase the number of points they can use (partners, groups of three or four).
2. Introduce hoops or ropes which can be used to balance in new and different ways.
3. Alternate the children calling out the number of points.
4. Decide what is the hardest way to balance on a specific number of points. What is the easiest?
5. Change from three points to two points without falling, then four to three, five to four.
6. Have children balance on the number of points specified on cards held up by the teacher.

7. Have children balance on the number of points corresponding
    to the number of objects the teacher holds.

Machines
Other skill development: flexibility, balance, coordination
Building machines with their own bodies provides children with
the opportunity to use their imaginations. They will create crazy,
funny body machines with a surprising array of sound effects if
given the opportunity. Machines can be built by an entire group,
individually, with partners, or in small groups. (See Figure 29.)

Begin by discussing moveable parts in engines. Explore the
various motions arms can make (bend, straighten, twist, etc.).

Figure 29   An "up and down" machine.

Also do leg, body, and head movement variations. Move only one body part in a specific way. Then have another child touch the first in some manner, and move a different body part. Add onto the machine. Have each child choose a specific sound for his or her movement (swish, hiss, clang, etc.).

Variations:

1. Vary the groupings.
2. Have only specific body-part machines (e.g., only head, or leg, or arm machines).
3. Make moving machines that roll, jump, run, and so on, but that do not lose their sound or special movements.
4. Try to make machines that look more like real machines (e.g., some children are the wheels moving their arms or rolling, others are the shovel in front of the tractor).
5. Make machines that are very quiet.
6. Make machines that have only big body parts (arms, legs) moving or only small parts (eyes, fingers, toes) moving.

Mirrors
Other skill development: body image, flexibility, laterality, directionality, eye-hand coordination
Body parts shadow one another as children mirror the movements made by you or other children. (See Figure 30.) The smallest body movements contrast with gross body movements. Right and left, forward and back, or side to side movements can be translated into mirror images as children learn through imitating. Begin by having all the children follow your movements while standing still.

Variations:

1. Have one child lead the group.
2. Have children choose partners; then work in groups of three or four.
3. Pair two groups with two groups.
4. Add moving across the floor to the motion to be mirrored.
5. Make a stationary model and have another group copy it.
6. Change the stance of someone in the group; then copy the form.
7. Place some children behind the image to be mirrored, others in front. Identify differences.

Figure 30   Children playing Mirrors.

Simon Says
Other skill development: auditory discrimination
One person is Simon, and children follow only Simon's directions that are accompanied by "Simon says." If a direction is taken that is not accompanied by "Simon says," the child traditionally is out. Instead of playing the game so that it excludes children (and, in most cases, those children who need the most practice are eliminated first), change the consequences of a wrong response to something like having the children simply correct their response. Or you might have two parallel games of "Simon Says" going on. When children give the wrong response, they go to the other game.
   Variations:

1. Use children's names rather than "Simon."
2. Vary groups and allow children to be callers.
3. Give group challenges—can several children identify specific body parts with each other?

4. Play "No, Simon." Do not do what Simon says, only what is not accompanied by "Simon says."
5. Vary the speed with which the caller gives out directions.
6. Play "Reverse Simon." Have children do what Simon says not to do.

Body Outline Drawings
Other skill development: laterality, directionality, form perception
The children work in pairs. One child in each pair lies down on large butcher paper and the other outlines his or her partner's body. Then they trade places. When both have a drawing, they color themselves.
    Variations:

1. Have the children place their feet, hands, and other body parts on their own drawings.
2. Have children place themselves and/or different body parts on their partner's drawing. Do they fit? How are they the same? How are they different?
3. Tape the pictures to the wall according to size, smallest to largest, with the feet touching the floor. Have the children match one another to the drawings. Each child may stand in front of someone else's drawing, trying to fit inside it.
4. Draw feet only, hands only. Have each child identify his or her own hand or foot.

Stand Up
Other skill development: balance, flexibility, coordination
Have children form pairs with their backs to one another. They hook elbows while seated and try to stand up together.
    Variations:

1. Going from standing to sitting.
2. Varying the size of the groups.

Body-Part Puzzles
Other skill development: spatial orientation, laterality, form perception, directionality, balance, flexibility
In this game children place one or more body-part cards in dif-

ferent patterns on the ground to create a body-part puzzle. They must first identify the symbols and then touch their own body parts to the correct cards and try to balance in stationary positions. Children can work alone or in small groups. The puzzles can be drawn on the board or put on poster boards and shown to the class, or merely presented randomly to the group. Body-part cards are shown in Figure 31. Left and right can be color-coded or marked with the initials *L* and *R*. Figure 32 shows some examples of body-part puzzles.

Variations:

1. Have children do some of the four puzzles.
2. Then have them make up their own. See the examples.
3. Make up some "Cannot" Puzzles.

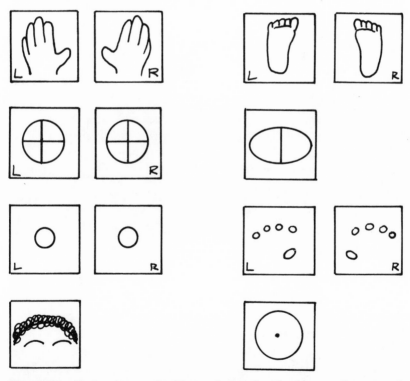

Figure 31 Body-part cards. First column: hands, knees, elbows, and forehead. Second column: feet, bottom, fingers, tummy.

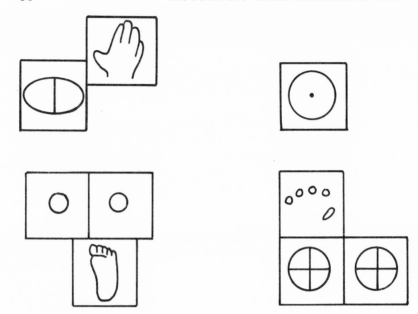

Figure 32   Four body-part puzzles.

Shadow Games
Other skill development: body image, balance, flexibility
Shadow games are fun outdoors when the sun is shining or in-
doors with a light against an inside wall. Have children take a
space where they can watch their shadows. Suggest moving
various body parts.
     Variations:

1. Make shadows big, small, wide, narrow and so forth. (See
   Figure 33.)
2. Make animal shadows as in Figure 34. Have children guess
   what they are.
3. Have children work in small groups or pairs to make animal-
   shadow machines, buildings, and other objects by combining
   their shadows, as in Figure 35.
4. Use only legs. Have children sit on the ground with their legs
   out swaying back and forth. What does the shadow look like?
   Then use arms only.

Figure 33   "How big can your shadow be?"

Figure 34   A shadow animal.

Figure 35   A three-headed monster.   59

Body-Part Walkabouts
Other skill development: spatial orientation, form perception,
laterality, directionality

This game is a dynamic version of Body-Part Puzzles. Rather than positioning themselves to balance on the body parts shown in the puzzles, children make walkabouts. Walkabouts are funny paths to follow created by drawing life-size symbols on separate pieces of 8 " × 11 " cardboard and placing the cards strategically on the floor. See the example in Figure 36. Children match their

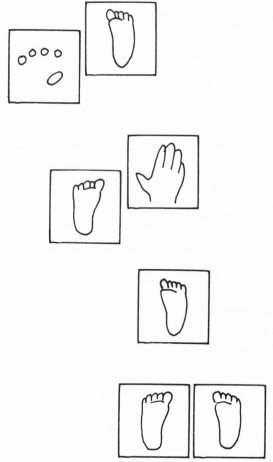

Figure 36   One path to follow.

appropriate body part to each symbol as they move along the walkabout.

The puzzles can start simple and become very complex. Children can work in pairs, teams, or individually. Having lots of body-part cards allows children to add more challenges to the game.

FUNDAMENTAL MOTOR PATTERNS

Running

Running games can be varied in speed, direction, and duration. Several group games involve running and are very enjoyable for young children. All running games help develop cardiovascular endurance.

Helpful Hint: Sometimes a few correcting words along with practice can help a child improve motor skill development. Through the process of exploring movement challenges, children learn about the various ways to move. They discover how to go fast and slow on toes and on heels. When practicing and playing, children need to continually rediscover how to run fast. During your continuing observations of this fundamental pattern, observe free-running situations carefully every two weeks, noting which movements need more reinforcement. Refer back to your observation checklist (see Appendix) to see how the children are changing over time. The hints in this and other sections lend themselves to "discovery" by children through guided problem-solving.

"CAN YOU?" CHALLENGES

1. Run: stretched high, crouched low, fast, slow, in a circle, on a line, with feet outside the line, on tiptoes, on heels, on sides of the feet, with long strides, with short steps, with knees high, with arms circling, using no arm swing, making big arm swings, with toes pointed.
2. Have children discover what the arms, legs, knees, and feet do in each of the various types of runs.
3. Combine speed, direction, and force variables as challenges. For example, run stretched high and fast, high and slow, high and in a circle, slow and zigzagging, fast and backwards, fast

and light, fast and heavy, slow and heavy, stretched high, and light and fast.
4. Run with others, matching running speeds. Children can run without touching anyone else, or groups of two or more can run holding hands. One child can run back to back with another.
5. Start and stop to signals (drum beat, bell-ringing, lights turned off, whistle) and freeze when stopped.

GAMES FOR RUNNING

The following games for running should be approached with the understanding that children will be at different levels in terms of understanding the games. Children will often not play by the correct rules, but they probably will have a wonderful time. Teach the correct rules when you introduce a game, but do not be surprised if the game evolves with a different set of rules as the children play. Play it as they play. The children may, with your help, alter the rules later, closer to the original game.

Some of the concepts children must learn in order to play tag games correctly involve distinguishing between what it means to be "It" versus not "It," the difference between tagging and being tagged, the need to run away from "It," and what is meant by safe areas. Even after playing many different forms of the same game, children may be confused. They may stand around after being tagged or run to be tagged instead of running away. They will learn the rules in time.

For most of these games, at least four children are needed to play. A group of ten is probably the maximum number you should play with.

Freeze Tag
Other skill development: reaction time, starting and stopping, balance, endurance, speed
One person is "It." "It" tries to catch the others. When tagged, a child must freeze. Other children may touch the frozen child to free him or her. Change who is "It" every minute until each child has had a turn.
    Variations:

1. Have children run holding hands with another child.
2. Change the boundaries.
3. Change the time span.
4. Make two children "It."
5. Have everyone move in slow motion.

Color (or Number, Shape, or Letter) Run
Other skill development: auditory discrimination,
reaction time, speed
Each child receives a colored piece of cardboard (or letters or numbers or shapes) which they sit on in a circle. One person calls out a color. Those children with that color run to a specific spot and back.
    Variations:

1. Call two colors together.
2. Have the children run to a different spot.
3. Vary the time, space, or force of the running pattern.

One, Two, Button My Shoe
Other skill development: auditory processing, changing
directions, cardiovascular endurance
In this game two parallel lines must be identified. One line is for the children to stand on; the other, for them to run to. One child is the caller and stands away from the rest of the group. The following rhyme must be learned before the game is attempted.

Children	*Caller*
One, two,	button my shoe.
Three, four,	close the door.
Five, six,	pick up sticks.
Seven, eight,	run or you'll be late!

The children and caller exchange responses. When the children hear the word *late*, they run to the other line and back. Whoever gets back first is the new caller.
    Variations:

1. Use a circle to run around.
2. Have children run backwards, fast, slowly, and so on.
3. Let the slowest runner become the caller.

Safe Tag
Other skill development: balance, spatial orientation, endurance, speed, agility
This is a tag game that has a specific safe object or body position. Children are safe and *cannot* be tagged if they touch a specific tree or pole; or if they pose in a specific way—standing on one leg, touching elbow to knee, standing back to back with another child, and so on.
   Variations:

1. Increase the number of "Its."
2. Have the caller vary the time, space, and force of the run.
3. Change the safe spot or position frequently.

Ships in the Harbor
Other skill development: running with a partner, stopping, starting, cardiovascular endurance
The children hold hands, forming one big circle. Two children who are outside the circle are the lost ship looking for a harbor. As they hold hands, they move around the outside of the circle. They choose a harbor by touching the joined hands of two children in the circle. The "ship" children must then run around the circle holding hands while the two "harbor" children hold hands and run in the opposite direction around the circle. The last pair to return to the harbor becomes the lost ship.
   Variations:

1. Vary the time, space, and force of the run.
2. Change the number of children who are the lost ship.
3. Have one person of each pair run inside the circle and one outside.
4. Have the other children in the circle move around together as the ship tries to find a harbor.

Go Tag
Other skill development: stopping/starting, agility, cardiovascular endurance, speed, directionality
All the players begin by standing or squatting in a line. The child at the head of the line is the runner; the child at the end of the line the chaser. On the signal to go, the chaser tries to catch the runner.

They run in the same direction, designated beforehand, around the line of children, as in Figure 37. At any time the chaser may tap another child on the shoulder and say "Go." The new child continues the chase, and the child who just finished running stands or squats down in the new runner's place. Once the runner is caught, he or she chooses a new runner, and the chaser picks a new chaser.

Variations:

1. Experiment with strategies on how to catch the runner.
2. Pair the children in the line so there are two runners and two chasers.
3. Change the number of children in the line. Have several short lines or a couple of medium-length lines rather than one long line.
4. Vary the running speed, space, or force (e.g., hard or light).

Walking

Children experiment with walking on their own. In groups the joy of discovery is enhanced by the others involved.

Figure 37 Four year olds playing Go Tag.

"CAN YOU?" CHALLENGES

1. Walk: on tiptoes; on heels; then alternate on tiptoes and heels.
2. Walk with long steps, with tiny steps.
3. Walk very tall, very small.
4. Take heavy steps, light ones.
5. Walk in a zigzag, backwards.
6. Walk next to someone without touching; walk with a partner, one walking forward, one walking backward; walk to the right, to the left; walk matching feet with a partner, right with right and left with left.
7. Wiggle the body while walking.
8. Walk fast; slow; fast, slow, fast.
9. Decide when walking becomes running.
10. Walk with arms overhead, with arms circling.
11. Walk with head nodding side to side.
12. Walk with four other children, all matching right feet and left feet.
13. Walk very softly, very hard.
14. Walk with the eyes closed.

GAMES FOR WALKING

Any of the games suggested in the section on running can be varied by having children walk instead of run.

Jumping

Jumping skills can be enhanced through practice and new challenges. The incentive to jump often comes from having something to reach for, jump over, or jump down from. Objects to be reached can be hung from strings; objects to be jumped over may be lined up to encourage jumping. Steps of varying heights offer wonderful opportunities for children to jump from. These activities encourage the development of strength and cardiovascular endurance.

Helpful Hints: Children may have difficulties jumping because they don't push off the ground. They may need to bend their knees more. Encourage children to use their arms to keep from losing their balance.

"CAN YOU?" CHALLENGES

1. Jump one (two, four, six) time(s).
2. Jump high, low, far.
3. Jump many times.
4. Hold arms way back and jump.
5. Jump fast, slowly.
6. Jump and turn.
7. Touch the toes while jumping, first putting legs in front of body, then behind.
8. Wiggle the legs while jumping.
9. Jump with eyes closed.
10. Jump with legs together, apart, then alternately together and apart.
11. Clap under the legs while jumping.
12. Jump with one partner, two partners.
13. Jump and touch both hands to both knees with legs bent, with legs straight.
14. Bend the knees and push off very hard.
15. See how far children can go in three jumps.

Variations:

1. Combine jumping with other movement patterns—walking, running.
2. Introduce equipment to be used to stimulate jumping, such as hoops, ropes, tires, steps. (See "Moving with Equipment," Chapter Five.)
3. Jump onto different surfaces like sand, grass, mats.

GAMES FOR JUMPING

Balloon Jumpers
Other skill development: eye-hand coordination, muscle strength, flexibility
Hang balloons of different colors from strings at varying heights in different areas of the playground or gym. Make sure that all

the children can reach at least two of them. Challenge children to run to the balloons in a specific sequence (yellow, red, blue), jump, and lightly tap the balloons in order. Have cardboard tubes or sticks available for children who can't reach the highest balloons when jumping by themselves.

Variations:

1. Change the order of the balloon taps.
2. Pair the children. Have them challenge another pair to a sequence of balloon taps.
3. Vary the time, space, and force of the jumps.
4. Change what the children must do to get from balloon to balloon (walk, hop, etc.).
5. Jump and tap the balloons while holding hands with a partner.

Crossing the Stream
Other skill development: perceptual skills, muscle strength
Children like to jump over water, and pretending is often just as much fun as the real thing. Use chalk to draw several sets of two lines that start out touching and angle away from each other, as shown in Figure 38.

Variations:

1. Jump across the stream. Mark the place where each child can jump across starting on two feet and landing on two feet.
2. Find the widest place each child can jump across.
3. Leap across, one foot to the other foot.
4. Jump across backwards.
5. Hop across on one foot.

Leap Frog
Other skill development: agility, muscle strength
This time-honored game needs no equipment and is enjoyable for an extended age range. Traditionally, the game is played by placing children in a widely spaced line. They have their heads down and are on their knees. The child at the end of the line jumps over each child in the line by placing his or her hands on each child's back and then jumping over the child. After the first child

Figure 38 Crossing the Stream. The "stream" should be approximately four feet at its widest point.

finishes jumping over the entire line, the child now left at the end leaps over everyone. Saying "Ribbit, ribbit" or "Croak, croak" with each jump adds a lot of fun and giggling.

Variations:

1. Speed up the leaps by having each child get up to leap as soon as he or she has been jumped over.
2. Play Leap Frog backwards.
3. Have children use only one hand to push off.
4. Space the line of children so that the jumper must do a specified number of jumps before reaching each child to leap over.

Throwing and Catching

Throwing and catching activities go together as clearly as children and movement. Children receive great satisfaction from throwing objects of all sizes and shapes. Spoons, balls, cups, and plates are all fair game. Children's fascination with watching objects go up and come down seems endless. Perceptual skills involving eye-hand coordination are the major component in throwing and catching.

Helpful Hints: The biggest problem children have with catching is that they do not look at the ball as it comes to them. Encourage them to do so. In addition, to improve their throwing accuracy, encourage them to have their hand(s) pointed to the target they are throwing to.

"CAN YOU?" CHALLENGES

1. Throw the ball up into the air using two hands, using the right hand, using the left hand.
2. Bounce it and catch it.
3. Throw it high, low.
4. Roll it. Spin it on the floor. Roll it along a line. Roll it with short pushes around the circle. Roll it and run to catch it.
5. Bounce the ball, turn around, and catch it. Bounce it, clap two times, and catch it.
6. Bounce it into a circle. Bounce it against the wall and catch it.
7. Bounce the ball to a partner. Bounce it and turn before the partner catches it.
8. Throw it high, turn, and catch it.
9. Put a top spin on the ball, a side spin, a back spin. (See Figure 39 for examples.)
10. Throw the ball up and catch it gently.
11. Throw the ball through a hoop, at a target, at a clown's face.
12. Toss the ball from one hand to the other.
13. Bounce it while walking, running.
14. Bounce it and walk without bumping into anyone.
15. Decide what texture of ball is easiest to catch, hardest.
16. Decide what size ball is easiest to catch, hardest.

Figure 39   From left to right, top spin, side spin, and back spin.

17. See if children can catch with their arms stiff, bent.
18. See what happens when the children catch with stiff fingers.
19. Watch how the children move when they catch.
20. Throw without moving the feet.
21. While throwing, move the foot opposite the throwing hand.
22. Try to catch with the eyes closed. Decide how you can learn to catch with your eyes closed. Figure out what the eyes do when you catch.

Variations:

1. Use different sizes and textures of objects (tennis balls, Nerf balls, smooth plastic balls, beach balls, balloons, bean bags, playground balls, rolled-up socks).
2. Change the groupings of children if the class has been divided.
3. Have groups of children display simple ball skills to share with other groups.
4. Invent a simple game to share with other groups.
5. Introduce new equipment like hoops, ropes, targets, tires to throw balls into or at.

GAMES FOR THROWING AND CATCHING

Limit your expectations initially for any of the throwing and catching games. Very young children will have great difficulty in stopping the ball because of their level of immaturity in these fundamental patterns. Older children, depending on their experience and maturation, will have greater success. Working with small groups of children for short but frequent periods during a week will give children the best opportunity to improve their ball-handling skills.

Ball Pass
Other skill development: ball-handling, eye-hand coordination
Children stand in a circle and push the ball along the ground to the hands of the next child. (See Figures 40 and 41.) Soon another ball is introduced, then another, and another until several balls are moving around the circle at once.
  Variations:

1. Have the children bounce the ball to the next child.
2. Have children clap or jump when they do not have a ball.

Figure 40   A group of four year olds playing Ball Pass. The children are jumping as the ball is pushed along the ground to another player.

Figure 41 Three year olds playing a simpler game of Ball Pass.

3. Have children roll the ball across the circle to someone.
4. Vary the size of the groups and the numbers of balls.
5. Turn every other child around so that children alternate facing in and out of the circle.
6. Have a small circle inside the larger circle.
7. Vary the types of balls used.
8. Vary the type of throw.
9. Pass the ball directly into the hands of the next child.

Hit the Clown
Skill development: throwing, eye-hand coordination
Make several clown targets with chalk or on big pieces of cardboard like the example in Figure 42. Have each child try to hit the clowns' eyes, ears, nose, mouth, hat, or cheeks.
Variations:

1. Vary the types of balls used.
2. Draw different clowns.

Figure 42   Clown target.

3. Have the children move farther and farther away from the clown as they throw.
4. Vary the type of throw (underhand, two hands, overhead, one hand).

Throwers and Catchers
Other skill development: eye-hand coordination, running
Arrange the children, one behind the other, in two lines that are about five feet apart, with the lines facing each other. The first child in one line is given the ball to throw to the first child in the opposite line. As soon as the child throws the ball, he or she runs to the end of his or her own line. Each child takes a turn passing the ball to the child across and running to the end of the line. The goal is to have each child catch and throw the ball without letting the ball escape.
    Variations:

1. Vary the type of throws that children use.
2. Vary the way children move to the end of the line.
3. Try the game in two circles, one inside the other.
4. Use various sizes and types of balls or bean bags.
5. Have each child use a type of throw that is different from those used by the other children.

Stop Ball
Other skill development: eye-hand coordination, auditory discrimination
The children stand in a big circle. One child is the caller and stands in the center with a blindfold or hands over his or her eyes. The children pass the ball around the circle. Whenever the caller decides to, he or she calls "Stop ball," and the child holding the ball becomes the new caller.
 Variations:

1. Try the game using more than one ball.
2. Have children bounce the ball around the circle.
3. Change the direction of the passes.
4. Vary the types of throws and catches.
5. Add a movement such as two high jumps when a child receives the ball.

Kicking

The rapid growth in the popularity of soccer in the United States has spurred many young children to imitate their older brothers, sisters, or parents. Since most kicking activities also involve running after the ball, they definitely promote development of the cardiovascular system.

"CAN YOU?" CHALLENGES

1. Kick the ball with one foot, the other foot, both feet together.
2. Push the ball forward touching it only with the inside of each foot, the outside of each foot.
3. Pull the ball along touching it only with the soles of the feet.
4. Kick the ball to a partner.
5. Kick the ball forward while running.
6. Balance the ball on top of the foot.
7. Kick the ball when it is rolled to you.
8. Push the ball around a circle.
9. Push the ball in different directions.

10. Kick the ball with the heel.
11. Drop the ball from the hands and kick it.
12. Kick the ball through a hoop.
13. Kick the ball between two cones.
14. Kick the ball to the wall.
15. Stop the ball with the inside of the foot, with the outside of the foot.
16. See how high the children can kick the ball.
17. Figure out what part of the foot is used when the ball is kicked the highest.

Variations:

1. Use different size balls, balloons.
2. Change groupings of children to pairs, small groups.
3. Use obstacles to kick around and targets to kick at.

GAMES FOR KICKING

All the games in the throwing and catching section can be adapted to develop the skill of kicking. The precautions in that section about limiting your expectations for success at these games apply to kicking as well. These games will be more successful with older children who have developed reasonably good kicking skills.

Wallopers
Other skill development: catching, eye-hand and eye-foot coordination, agility
Divide the children into two groups. Each group stands on opposite sides of a long line and about five feet from it. One child places the ball on the ground and kicks it across the line. The opposite group tries to stop the ball by catching it. Whoever catches it kicks it back. No child may kick the ball a second time until each child on the team has had a turn.

Variations:

1. Change the size of the groups.
2. Introduce more balls.
3. Use different size balls.
4. Change the boundaries of the games.

5. Vary the kind of movement children must do to get to the ball
   (i.e., jump to reach the ball, skip to reach the ball).

Crazy Legs
Other skill development: eye-foot coordination,
cardiovascular endurance
Children stand in a big circle, spaced about an arm's length from
one another. One child is chosen to be "Crazy Legs." Crazy Legs
kicks the ball around the outside of the circle. (See Figure 43.) At
any time Crazy Legs may kick the ball into the middle of the circle and then tap another child on the back. He or she then begins
to chase Crazy Legs who is running around the circle. The tapped
child tries to catch Crazy Legs before the latter gets back to
the empty space in the circle. If Crazy Legs is caught, he or
she returns to the circle and the game continues with the new
Crazy Legs.
   Variations:

1. Have Crazy Legs weave in and out between the children in the
   circle as he or she kicks the ball.

Figure 43   Three year olds playing Crazy Legs.

2. Add a movement that the children in the circle must do while the chase is on (i.e., jump in place as high as possible, jump and turn).
3. Have a Crazy Leg pair who must kick the ball between them as they move around the circle.
4. Change the number of Crazy Legs and chasers.
5. Use a line instead of a circle.

Rope Kickers
Other skill development: eye-foot coordination, ball control
Children are divided into two teams. A rope is stretched out on the ground between the two teams, and two children are chosen to stand at the ends of the rope to serve as "caretakers." Each team lines up five yards behind the rope, as illustrated in Figure 44. The object is to have one child from each team successfully kick the ball over the rope in succession. The children go to the end of their team line following their turn to kick. When two children are successful, the caretakers raise the rope about a foot. Both teams work together to raise the rope as high as they can.
   Variations:

1. Vary the distance between the teams and the rope.
2. Change the group size.
3. Use different types of balls.
4. Change the way children must move to get to the end of the line.

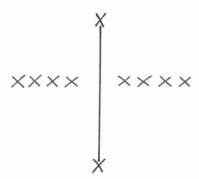

Figure 44 Floor plan for Rope Kickers.

Snuffers

Other skill development: eye-foot coordination, balance

In this game, children stand in a circle with hands clasped or arms entwined, and a ball is kicked into the middle. Without letting go, children must kick the ball but keep it in the circle. Often the circle will have to move as a group to keep the ball inside.

Variations:

1. Vary the number of children per circle.
2. Vary the number of balls.
3. Alternate the children so that some face into the circle and some face out.

5

Moving with Equipment

Fundamental motor patterns can be enhanced through the use of many different kinds of equipment. Balls, hoops, ropes, tires, bean bags, balance boards, and beams are only some of the many kinds of equipment children can use.

Balls

Since balls can be bounced, rolled, thrown, caught, and spun, as well as thrown at and into things, they are an important component in a motor activity program aimed at developing eye-hand coordination.

The size and texture of balls change the complexity of the task. Small balls are easier to throw, but large balls are easier to catch. Spongy soft balls like Nerf balls are easier to catch than similarly sized harder balls. Balls made of sponge, yarn, wadded newspapers, or rolled socks help children learn to catch by eliminating the fear of getting hurt.

BALL BALANCING FUN
Using any type of ball, have children work together in groups of two to move while they hold the ball between them without using their hands. They may balance it between their foreheads, stomachs, hips, or shoulders. Move across the yard and back.

Variations:

1. Sit down and then stand up without losing the ball.
2. Use several balls or balloons.
3. Vary the movement pattern.

4. Pass the ball to another pair of children.
5. Increase the number of children in each grouping.

Note: Other ball challenges are developed in "Throwing and Catching" in Chapter 4.

Hoops and Tires

Hoops and tires can be used as large targets. They can be rolled and balanced on, moved through and around, and placed in different configurations on the ground. Spatial relationships are reinforced by moving the body in relation to a hoop or tire.

"CAN YOU?" CHALLENGES

1. Roll the hoop across the yard without letting it fall.
2. Make it spin like a top.
3. Move through a hoop when it is rolling.
4. Roll the hoop so it comes back to you.
5. Use the hoop to jump with as if it were a rope.
6. Throw it in the air and catch it.
7. Make the hoop turn around the waist, the neck.
8. Roll a hoop or tire along a line.
9. Whirl the hoop on the arm.
10. Roll it to a partner.
11. Walk in it with a partner.
12. Put it on the ground and jump around it. Jump in and out of it. (See Figure 45.) Jump with one foot in and one foot out.
13. Jump through a series of hoops (or tires) without touching any. Hop through them. Run through them.
14. Walk around the top without falling off. Walk around backwards.
15. Roll the hoop (or tire) as slowly as it will go without falling.
16. Bounce a ball inside it.
17. Throw a ball through it.
18. Pick up the hoop without bending the knees.
19. Hold it over the head and drop it so it doesn't touch any part of the body.
20. Bounce the ball to a partner so that it lands inside the hoop.

Figure 45 Jumping into a hoop, a "Can You?" Challenge.

GAMES

Insiders
Skill development: running, jumping, cardiovascular
endurance, spatial orientation
All the hoops or tires are placed on the ground. Children stand outside the hoops. On the command "Go" the children run around the area without touching anyone or the hoops. On the word "hoopers," each child must find the nearest hoop to jump into. Only one child can be in a hoop. (See Figure 46.)
   Variations:

1. Change the movement pattern children use to get into the hoop.
2. Add something to what they must do in the hoop (e.g., balance on one foot).
3. Use half the number of hoops and have children run in pairs.

Figure 46   Three year olds playing Insiders.

Hoop or Tire Tag
Skill development: cardiovascular endurance, running, spatial orientation, balance
In this tag game the hoops or tires are "free" zones. Use half the number of hoops as children who are playing. Only one child can be in a free zone at a time. If a child is in a hoop or tire, he or she must leave when another child comes. One child is "It" and can tag children who are not in the free zone. As children are tagged, they too become "It." The last child tagged becomes "It" for the next game.
   Variations:

1. Change the movement patterns from running to perhaps sliding, galloping, or jumping.
2. Vary the number of free zones.
3. Add something for the children to do while in the free zone—balance on one hand and one foot.
4. Have the children hold the free zones upright: they must fit themselves in and hold the hoop or tire up.

Musical Hoops
Skill development: running, spatial orientation, auditory discrimination

Like the traditional Musical Chairs, this game gradually reduces the number of hoops to be selected; however, it does not eliminate children. In this game children work in pairs, and each pair has one large hoop that they stand inside, holding it up at waist level. When the music (or hand clapping or drum beating) starts, the children run around the room together, staying inside their hoop. When the music stops, each pair must join with another pair inside both their hoops held together. The game continues until no more children can fit inside the hoops.

Variations:

1. Change the movement pattern—jump, hop, slide, etc.
2. Place the hoops on the ground and have the children jump inside them when the music stops. Remove a hoop each time so that more and more children must get into the remaining hoops.

Ropes

Since ropes can be made into many shapes, they can be changed to promote many interesting movement patterns. They are particularly useful in reinforcing spatial awareness, laterality, and directionality, as well as in promoting agility, strength, and cardiovascular endurance. They also aid in pattern recognition.

"CAN YOU?" CHALLENGES
These challenges get progressively more difficult. The skills required to do these tasks build gradually.

1. Stretch a rope out like a line, like a circle.
2. Walk around the rope circle.
3. Balance on top of the circle.
4. Jump back and forth across the rope without touching it.
5. Make the rope into a letter, into a number.
6. Do two jumps on one side of the rope, then two on the other, and keep this up.
7. Try moving backwards along the rope.

8. Run around the rope so it always stays on your right.
9. Figure out how many different ways you can jump over the rope.
10. Hold the rope in each hand and jump over it as it swings.
11. Hold one end of the rope, swing it low around yourself in a circle, and jump over it as it reaches your feet.

GROUP ACTIVITIES

Building Blocks
Skill development: jumping, spatial orientation, flexibility, strength
Lay a long rope on the ground. Have all the children jump over it. Raise it about two inches. Have the children go over it again. Continue to raise the rope until no one can get over it. Then begin to lower the rope and have the children duck under it until no one can do it. The children try not to touch the rope.

Variations:

1. Vary the movement pattern and change the distance children must cover to get to the rope and over it.
2. Have children work in pairs.
3. Play the game jumping backwards.
4. Wiggle the rope.

Reachers
Skill development: strength, eye-hand coordination
This game is similar to Building Blocks, except that children must try to jump up to reach the rope, rather than pass over or under it. The beginning level for the rope is one foot over the average height of the class. It is raised a little bit after each jump until no one can reach it. Then it is lowered a little bit after each jump, until it is within reach of the entire class again.

Variations:

1. Put the rope on a slant and have children try different parts of the rope.
2. Vary the movement patterns used to approach the rope.
3. Add a turn to the jump-and-reach motion.
4. Vary the groups.

Bean Bags

Bean bags are easy to catch because of their flexible shape. They are invaluable for developing early catching skills and can aid in learning to identify body parts and in the development of laterality and eye-hand and eye-foot coordination.

"CAN YOU?" CHALLENGES

1. Throw the bean bag high.
2. Throw and catch it from one hand to the other.
3. Walk with it on your head, shoulder.
4. Run with it on your head.
5. Balance two bean bags, one on each foot, as you walk.
6. Throw a bean bag over your shoulder, turn, and catch it.
7. Play catch with a partner.
8. Throw it to a partner under your arm, under your leg, between your legs.
9. Throw two bean bags, one in each hand, into the air and catch them.
10. Throw two bean bags with a partner.
11. Swing one leg while balancing the bean bag on top of the foot.
12. Throw bean bags through targets.
13. Balance a bean bag on one foot and toss it up to catch it.
14. Jump holding it between the knees.

GAMES

Target games using hoops, tires, and so forth, are fun for children. A game similar to horseshoes can be played in which children on each team try to toss the bean bag as close to a particular spot as possible.

One Step is a game in which two children face each other. They try to throw the bean bag to each other without the catcher moving their feet. Each time they are successful, they each take one step back and try again. The goal is to see how far they can get from each other while successfully completing the throw and catch. If a player has to move his or her feet, both players return to the starting position.

Balance Beams and Boards

Balance is specific to each task and type of equipment. The skill required to move along a balance beam is distinct from the kind necessary to be successful on an unstable balance board that has a rocker-type bottom. A balance beam is a long board that varies in width. It is held securely in one place by two blocks, one at each end. It is important for children to have balancing experiences with all kinds of equipment. Of course, wide beams are easier to walk on than narrow ones, and eye-level visual targets at both ends of a beam make balancing easier.

"CAN YOU?" CHALLENGES ON THE BEAM

1. Walk across the beam.
2. Crawl across the beam.
3. Scoot across on your bottom.
4. Move across using hands and feet.
5. Walk along the beam stepping up onto the beam with one step, down off the beam with the next step, back up again, and so forth.
6. Walk heel to toe.
7. Walk backwards.
8. Walk forward, turn in the middle, and then walk backwards to the end of the beam.
9. Walk across with feet turned sideways.
10. Pick up a bean bag that is resting on the beam.
11. Balance a bean bag on your head as you go across.
12. Walk to the center and be an airplane.
13. Walk to the middle, bounce, and then continue.
14. Balance on one foot.
15. Walk with another child holding hands, one moving forward, one moving backwards.
16. Play catch with a bean bag while standing on the beam.
17. Try walking on the beam with different arm positions—out to the side, over the head, on the hip, behind the back, folded across the chest. Decide which is easiest.
18. Walk across with eyes closed.

"CAN YOU?" CHALLENGES ON THE BALANCE BOARD

1. Balance the board while looking at a target.
2. Balance with eyes closed.
3. Turn around on the board.
4. Toss a bean bag and catch it while balancing.
5. Jump on the board.
6. Touch knees, toes, eyes, head while on the board.
7. Balance on the toes, on the heels.
8. Balance on one hand and one foot.
9. Try the arms in various positions.
10. Try various foot positions: heel to toe; feet crossed, wide apart, close together.
11. Tilt the body to the back, then to the front.
12. Tilt the body to the left and right.
13. Balance with a partner on the board.
14. Kneel down and stand back up.

Mat Activities

Young children can do simple stunts on mats, grass, or carpeted areas to practice non-locomotor movement patterns.

STUNTS

Log Roll
Children lie on their backs stretching their bodies with hands clasped over the head. Then they roll to the right and left.

Egg Roll
Lying on their backs, children bring the knees up to the chest, clasp them with the arms, and then roll in all possible directions.

Seat Circle
Children sit on the floor with knees bent, feet off the floor, and hands braced behind them. Then they spin to the left and to the right. They may try to balance a bean bag on their heads or to keep it between their knees.

Turk Stand
Standing with arms crossed, children cross their legs and sit down. Then they stand back up without changing arm or foot position.

Thread the Needle
Children clasp their hands in front of their bodies; then they try to step through their clasped hands with each foot. Leaving hands together, they then try to step back.

GROUP ACTIVITIES

Slithery Snake
Skill development: directionality, spatial orientation, strength, flexibility
Divide children into pairs and have them stretch out on their stomachs. One child in each pair holds the ankles of his or her partner. Then they slither like a snake across the floor and attach themselves to another pair to make a four-child snake. Keep blending snakes together until there is only one giant slithery snake, as in Figure 47.
   Variations:

1. Try rolling over together with a two-child snake, then with a four-child, eight-child, or longer snake.
2. Have the snake coil and uncoil.
3. Set up hills (rolled-up carpeting or mats) for the snake to move over.

Bouncing Ball
Skill development: eye-hand coordination, kinesthesis, sequencing
Each child stands in front of a partner and tries to bounce and roll the other child like a ball. The partner must bounce and roll on cue.

Wring the Dish Rag
Skill development: flexibility, spatial orientation
Two children hold hands, facing each other. They try to do a full

Figure 47   Children playing Slithery Snake outdoors.

turn by raising one pair of arms and then the other, but without letting their hands separate.

Roly-Poly
Skill development: spatial orientation, directionality, laterality
Children lie on the mat next to one another. The child on the end rolls over the top of the other children to the end. Each child follows in turn.

Animal Walks
Skill development: flexibility, strength, coordination

1. Puppy dog. On hands and knees, move the alternate leg and hand forward at the same time.
2. Bear Walk. On hands and knees, move the hand and foot on the same side of the body forward together as in Figure 48.
3. Seal Walk. Lying on the stomach, push up with the arms so that the head and chest are raised and supported on straight arms. Move the arms forward one at a time while dragging the legs behind, as shown in Figure 49.

Figure 48   An exaggerated Bear Walk.

Figure 49   The Seal Walk.

Figure 50   The Crab Walk.

4. Crab Walk. From a sitting position, put the hands behind the
   body and push up onto the hands and feet. (See Figure 50.)
   Move around the room.
5. Frog Jump. Squat, placing the hands on the floor *between* the
   knees. Spring up and land back on all fours, as in Figure 51.
6. Elephant Walk. Bend over at the waist and clasp both hands
   together, keeping the arms straight. Swing the arms back and
   forth like a trunk while lumbering along.
7. Rabbit Hop. Squat, placing the hands on the floor outside the
   knees. Reach forward with both hands, then jump to bring the
   feet to the hands. Reach the hands out again and jump toward
   the hands, as shown in Figure 52.
8. Lame Puppy. The children choose a hurt "paw" and move
   around the room on hands and knees without using the injured
   paw. (See Figure 53.)

Figure 51 The Frog Jump. The boy in front has forgotten to put his hands inside his knees, rather than outside.

Figure 52 The Rabbit Hop. These children like to move on their knees, rather than on their feet.

Figure 53   The Lame Puppy.

Obstacle Courses

The value of obstacle courses is that they bring many movement patterns together in one activity, while being fun and creative. They are also invaluable in teaching sequencing. Initially, you may set up the obstacle courses, but with experience and practice the children will become more able to make decisions and to solve problems. They can then invent a course on their own. You may suggest a problem such as, "Try to improve your jumping height." Several groups of students can then use the available equipment to set up their own challenge courses.

Any equipment in the area is fair game for obstacle courses: trash cans, ropes, hoops, tires, benches, chairs, and rugs are all suitable. Directions on how to go through the course can be open-ended (e.g., "Do something at each new obstacle"), or they can be specific (e.g., "Move under the table, jump the rope, go to the right of the chair, and hop back to the start").

Have several courses set up or an alternative activity going so that children do not have to wait long periods of time between turns. Some ideas for courses are illustrated in Figure 54.

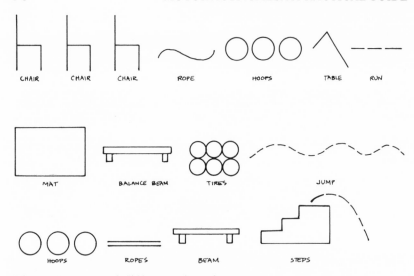

Figure 54   Several different obstacle courses.

Other Types of Equipment

1. *Blankets* can be used for children to roll up in, for pulling children along, for putting on top of children so they can collectively move underneath, for supporting children when held by adults, or for supporting balls, balloons, or bean bags.
2. *Scoops* cut from plastic milk containers are great for catching skills.
3. *Streamers* of ribbons or newspaper strips are fun to run with, jump over, and make moving patterns with.
4. Bicycle *inner tubes* make elastic pulleys.
5. *Scooter boards* can be used in many ball games or for the sheer joy of the rapid movement that they provide. They help develop upper shoulder strength when ridden on the stomach and abdominal strength when ridden while seated, as well as general coordination.

6

Moving Without Equipment

Imagery and rhythms provide impetus for movement, as do balls, ropes, and hoops. Giving young children the opportunity to create movement to words, thoughts, and music adds an aesthetic quality that is often lacking when movement is done with equipment.

Since materials in the area of imagery and rhythms for preschoolers are plentiful, this chapter will mention just a few activities, and then refer you to some of the abundant resources available.

"CAN YOU?" CHALLENGES STRESSING MOVEMENT QUALITIES

Moving Slowly
Can you move like

>> a snail?
>> a turtle?
>> a worm?
>> the sun coming up?
>> water dripping from a faucet?

Moving Quickly
Can you move like

>> a jet?
>> an arrow?
>> the wind?
>> a falling star?

Moving Heavily
Can you move like

> a car?
> a hippopotamus?
> an elephant?
> a locomotive?
> a large boulder?

Moving Lightly
Can you

> fall like a gentle raindrop?
> fly like Tinkerbell?
> float like a feather?
> wave gently like a leaf?

Being Straight
Can you make yourself into

> a tall tree?
> the letter *T?*
> a skyscraper?
> a pencil?
> a telephone pole?
> a line on the ground?
> a road?

Being Curved
Can you

> bounce like a ball?
> roll like a doughnut?
> roll across the floor like a marble?
> be the letter *C?*

MORE "CAN YOU?" CHALLENGES
Can you

> walk with your feet stuck in bubble gum?
> walk on slippery ice?

make yourself as small as a mouse?
make yourself as big as a house?
be a bird in flight?
get a flat tire?
throw a heavy rock?
be a spinning top?
stretch yourself like a rubber band?
be a strong wind blowing?
swim through a gooey, sticky swamp?
blow yourself up like a balloon and float away?
fly a kite?
climb a steep mountain?
swing from side to side like a tree in a gentle wind?
join together to make a moving car?

GROUP ACTIVITIES

Going on a Tiger Hunt
Skill development: auditory discrimination, sequencing
One person leads the group through the tiger hunt while all the children follow and repeat the phrases:

Leader: "I'm going on a tiger hunt."
Children: "I'm going on a tiger hunt."
Leader: "And I'm not afraid."
Children: "And I'm not afraid."
     (The children continue to repeat the phrases after the leader.)
"First I'll walk through the tall grass." *(Pretend to walk with big steps, pushing the grass to the sides.)*
"Then I'll climb up this big tree." *(Pantomime climbing.)*
"Now I'm climbing to the top of the steep hill." *(Pantomime.)*
"Whoops, I slid down the hill." *(Pantomime.)*
"Now I'll row my boat across this lake." *(Pantomime.)*
"Whoops, I have to swim across this river." *(Pantomime.)*
"Now I'm going into the cave quietly and carefully on tiptoe." *(Pantomime.)*
"Ooh! There's the tiger! Quick!" *(Pantomime the above actions in reverse order.)* "Swim across the river! . . . Row the boat! . . . Climb the hill! . . . Slide down! . . . Climb the tree! . . . Go back through the tall grass!"

Leader (out of breath):   "We went on a tiger hunt."
Children: "We went on a tiger hunt. And we were [or were not] afraid!"

Dramatize a Story or a Poem
Skill development: auditory discrimination, sequencing
Choose an adventure story or a poem that the children particularly enjoy and that stimulates interesting movement. Give children parts to act out as you read the story. "Little Red Riding Hood," "Where the Wild Things Are," "Peter and the Wolf," "The Little Engine That Could," and "The Three Billy Goats Gruff" are good stories for this activity.
   Variations:

1. Have a child tell the story but change the ending.
2. Change the setting or characters in the story.
3. Tell the story backwards and do all the actions in reverse.

Popcorn Game
Skill development: jumping, strength, endurance
All the children are pieces of popcorn. When they pop, they must jump and move around the play area. If they touch another child, the popcorn pieces stick together and must jump around together. Eventually all the children will be popping around as one huge popcorn ball.

Mulberry Bush
Skill development: auditory discrimination, sequencing,
fundamental motor patterns
This traditional circle game can be varied endlessly to accommodate children's creative imaginations. The children join hands in a circle and walk around singing the chorus:

   "Here we go 'round the mulberry bush, the mulberry bush,
      the mulberry bush.
   Here we go round the mulberry bush
   So early in the morning."

Following the chorus have the children stop walking and sing the traditional verses as they pretend to do household chores: "This is the way we wash our clothes . . . brush our teeth . . . mend our clothes." However, you could also try such verses as "This is the way we kick a ball . . . throw a ball . . . turn around . . . hammer a nail . . . ride a wave [sled] . . . roller-skate . . . ride a horse."

Variations:

1. Vary the movements the children do around the circle while the chorus is sung.
2. Have some children stand in place during the chorus while others move around by weaving in and out.

TRADITIONAL MOVEMENT SONGS

The library, bookstore, and record stores are wonderful resources for recordings of old favorites like "Old MacDonald Had a Farm," "The Hokey Pokey," "Row, Row, Row Your Boat," "Pop, Goes the Weasel," and "I've Been Working on the Railroad." There are also record catalogues like *Enrichment Material for the Entire Curriculum*, published by Children's Book and Music Center, 2500 Santa Monica Boulevard, Santa Monica, CA 90404.

Children's Television Workshop produces a series of "Sesame Street" records distributed by Muppets, Inc., Sesame Street Records, Division of Distinguished Productions, Inc., 1 Lincoln Plaza, New York, NY 10023. Many of the songs are movement activities that invite children to move along with the Sesame Street characters.

Hap Palmer has a series of records and songbooks that incorporate movement and learning. His materials can be ordered through many children's book or music stores.

7

Health, Heart, and Safety

Children usually are a healthy, hearty group. They challenge their hearts through the exercise that is a natural part of their being. Often children are not made aware of the benefits their play has on their own growth. Movement provides a wonderful opportunity to introduce simple science concepts to young children. In addition, it reinforces the concept that exercise is good for the heart and for health in general.

HEALTH AND THE HEART

In introducing the concept of heart rate at this age, the goal is merely to develop awareness. Learning to be aware of pulse rates will be a useful tool for children to have as they grow and are interested in monitoring the effects of training on their cardiovascular systems. The beginning knowledge and skills introduced to young children should help them establish lifelong values and attitudes toward their healthy bodies.

While adults are taught to take precise pulse rates, children can simply put their hands over their hearts to get a simple and direct measurement, as the child in Figure 55 is doing. Once you show children how to use their right hands to locate their hearts, they can experiment:

1. Find the heartbeat on your friends, family members, animals.
2. Learn to count when the teacher says, "Go" and to stop counting when the teacher says, "Stop."
3. Discover what activities make the heart go the fastest, the slowest.

Figure 55   A three year old feeling his heart beat after running.

4. Monitor your heart before and after activity sessions.
5. Discover your heart rate at various times of the day (e.g., when you first get to school, after outside time, at story time).

Some important points to emphasize include:

1. Heart rates change through the day depending on your activities.
2. A particular heart-rate count is neither good nor bad. It merely tells you something about yourself.
3. In order to make the heart strong, you need good food, plenty of rest, and a lot of exercise.
4. The heart is a muscle, and it must be exercised like all the other muscles in the body in order to grow stronger.
5. The doctor listens to the sounds your heart makes with a stethoscope. This is one way to tell how healthy you are.
6. Children's heart rates are faster (higher) than those of adults.

HEALTH AND SAFETY

One of the major causes of injuries to children is accidents. Playground equipment has the potential to be dangerous if it is improperly assembled, is in disrepair, or is used in dangerous ways. Young children need to be made aware of the possible hazards in the play yard. They can learn about care and maintenance of equipment. They may also be able to help with sanding rough areas on wooden climbing structures or balance beams, or help hammer in exposed nails. They can alternate turns being equipment scouts who check the equipment for danger spots.

It is extremely important that children use the equipment properly. Sometimes there can be a fine line between encouraging creative use of equipment and dangerous use. If children can be included in developing the safety rules for equipment use, they are often more diligent in obeying the rules. Their ability to help in the rule-making process will depend on their age and maturity. Four year olds are often very capable of coming up with good safety rules.

8

Playgrounds and Play Yards

CREATIVE PLAY SPACES

Young children spend a great amount of time outdoors. Parks and playgrounds in general have done a less than adequate job of providing stimulating public environments for children's play. Most play yards have swings, slides, some type of climbing apparatus, sand, and grass or asphalt. Some newer playgrounds have interesting wooden climbing structures. These do more to stimulate creative play than do swings and slides. However, practically all existing playgrounds fall short of providing the impetus for movement that is essential to a child's development because they are static. Children cannot change the equipment to challenge themselves and practice specific movements.

There is a great need for play spaces in which children are free to create and challenge their movement potential. Some bright hope is now emerging in the form of "adventure playgrounds," which have been organized by recreation facilities and interested parent groups around the United States. Many adults have precious childhood memories of playing in the vacant lot down the block. The adventure playground has essentially made that lot a safe place to play, because it simulates a vacant lot while providing a supervised play area where the equipment is safe. Adventure playgrounds are made up of an array of boards, planks, boxes, tires, ladders, and other "junk." Children use this equipment to create their own play space. In the process they challenge themselves and enhance their growth. This type of play area is a natural extension of what can happen in children's homes. For more information about adventure playgrounds, contact the American Adventure Play Association through your local recreation center, college recreation department, or local library.

If the only playground equipment available is static, how can you make the most of it?

1. Use the play yard as an obstacle course.
2. Challenge children to think of all the ways they can climb a ladder and come down a slide.
3. How many ways can they go up the slide and come down the ladder?
4. What can they jump over or slide under?
5. How many ways can they sit to swing on a swing?
6. Can they sit two, even three, on a swing?
7. Can they use the swing for a basket to throw a ball in?
8. What movements make the swing go?

By working with the children, you can change static playgrounds into interesting places for creative movement.

EQUIPMENT: MAKING AND BUYING

Small Equipment

Hoops can be purchased (traditional hula hoops), or they can be made by using ¾ " plumbing tubing with a ¾ " plastic or wooden dowel inside to join the tubing. Tape encircles the joined section of the hoop, as seen in Figure 56. The advantage of making your

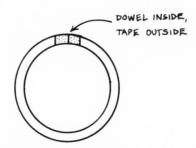

DOWEL INSIDE, TAPE OUTSIDE

Figure 56   A homemade hoop.

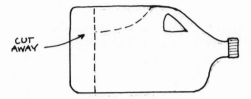

Figure 57 A bleach-bottle scoop.

own hoops is that you can make a variety of sizes. The standard-size hoop has an eight-foot circumference with a 1½ " dowel.

Scoops are useful for developing eye-hand coordination in catching. To make a scoop from an old bleach bottle, use scissors to cut off the bottom and make an opening slanting back toward the handle, as shown in Figure 57. Bleach bottles can also be used for boundary markers by filling the bottles half full with sand. They can be painted so they are easy to see.

Foam-rubber squares can be purchased in foam, upholstery, or mattress stores. As seen in Figure 58, numbers, letters, shapes, arrows (to indicate directions), and body-part codes can be painted on both their front and back. There are an endless variety of activities you and the children can develop with these soft squares. Carpet-square samples can be used in the same way.

Rope of various lengths can be purchased at local hardware stores. Number 12 sash cord works best.

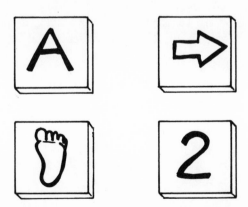

Figure 58 Squares can be made from foam rubber or carpet or cardboard.

Bean bags can be made out of old fabric sewn together into various shapes (circles, squares, rectangles, diamonds, triangles) and filled with beans, rice, or styrofoam chips. They, of course, are also available commercially.

Balls of various sizes, shapes, and textures are available in sporting good stores, as well as in local markets, drug stores, and variety stores.

Yarn balls can be made from one skein per ball. Wrap all the yarn around a piece of cardboard about five inches wide. Wrap a foot-long piece of twine or light cord loosely around the middle of the yarn a few times, and then slide out the cardboard. Next pull the twine tight and continue to wrap until you use it all. Tie the ends of the twine securely. Finally, cut through the loop ends on the ball and fluff them out. (See Figure 59.)

A sock ball can be made by stuffing the toe of an old sock with two double sheets of wadded-up newspaper. Twist the sock where the newspaper ends, and then push the sock back over the ball. Continue to twist and push until the sock is pulled back tightly. Finally, sew or tape the loose ends down.

Keep a healthy supply of balloons in several sizes with your small equipment. For variety, put small buttons inside before blowing them up to make them float unpredictably.

Tin-can stilts can be made from coffee cans. Drill two holes near the closed end of the can, and thread a rope through the holes so the children can hold the ropes as they walk with their feet on the closed end of the can. (See Figure 60.)

Traffic cones make excellent area markers for games and are also useful in setting up obstacle courses. Contact your state

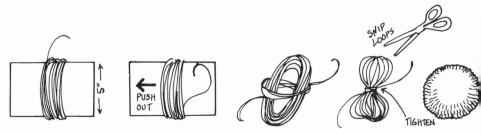

Figure 59   Yarn balls are easy to make.

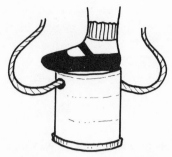

Figure 60   Coffee-can stilts.

police or local police department for possible free ones, or purchase them through sporting good outlets.

Discarded tires can be picked up at junk yards or gas stations. Bicycle shops generally give away old bicycle inner tubes that can be tied together to make stretch ropes or walking paths.

Larger Equipment

All of these pieces of equipment can be purchased commercially. However, homemade equipment is less expensive and just as effective. Some are relatively easy to make; others take more expertise.

Scooter boards are simply boards with four wheels. To make one, you will need ¾ " plywood cut either square (16 " × 16 ") or rectangular (16." × 24 ") with sanded edges and rounded corners. Screw in four casters, each placed 1½ inch diagonally from a corner. Tops can be carpeted if desired.

Balance beams can be made out of a 2 " × 4 " × 8 ' piece of lumber supported in removable stands that will accommodate the 4 " and the 2 " side of the beam. Of course, all edges should be sanded carefully. (See Figure 61.)

Balance boards can be constructed in several sizes and shapes. Square boards can be made from a 16 " × 16 " piece of ¾ " plywood by nailing a 2 " × 2 " block of wood to the middle of the large square, as in Figure 62. You can make rectangular boards (10 " × 24 ") by nailing to the board a 1 " × 1 " piece of wood running the width of the board, as shown in Figure 63. Cir-

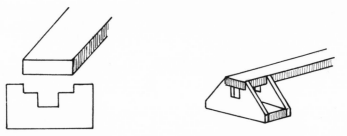

Figure 61 A balance beam with stands that will accommodate two board widths.

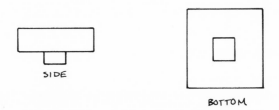

Figure 62 A square balance board.

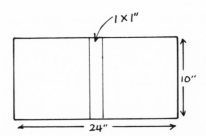

Figure 63 A rectangular balance board.

cular boards (14″ in diameter) with rocker bottoms can be made by nailing to the board two crossing half-circle supports, both with a 3″ radius and both cut at their radius so they fit together. Be sure to sand all boards, and put either carpeting or nonslip strips across their top.

Target cutouts are useful for target throws. They can be made by cutting out shapes (e.g., clown's faces, animals, numbers, names) in very heavy cardboard. The cutout spaces should be big enough to accommodate bean bags and small balls.

Stairs of several heights can be built into one piece of stationary equipment so that there are 4″, 6″, 10″, and 12″ risers for children to climb. See Figure 64.

A similar arrangement can be built using ladders, with rungs spaced at different intervals apart and at different incline levels. Figure 65 illustrates such a ladder arrangement.

Jumping tables of several sizes and heights can be stored inside one another. These tables should be made out of ¾″ plywood and the tops covered with carpet or nonslip strips. See Figure 66.

Old parachutes can sometimes be obtained through the military. However, blankets, sheets, or bedspreads can serve the same purpose. Cut a hole one foot in diameter in the center. Children can stand around the edges and shake it, make waves, roll balls or balloons to the center hole, or try to keep them out of the hole, run under the parachute, make tents or mushrooms, run with it, and have a great time thinking of new activities to do with it.

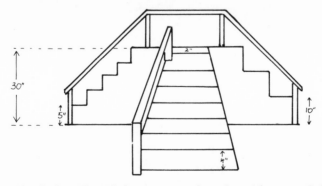

Figure 64 Stairs. The 6″ risers are on the other side, out of sight.

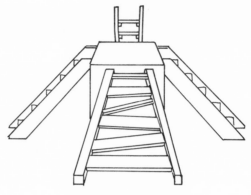

Figure 65   Ladders.

Yard Markings

Number and letter grids, 5 ′ × 5 ′, painted or chalked on the
ground like the ones illustrated in Figure 67, can be the impetus
for a number of interesting games. They can be used to reinforce
number and letter recognition and also to play math and word
recognition games. In addition, bean bags can be tossed in them,
they can be jumped in, and balance puzzles can be done in them,
plus a variety of other activities.

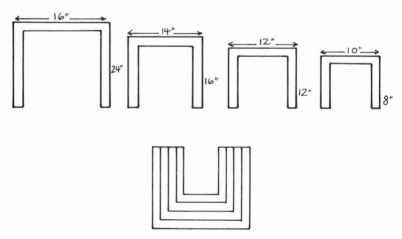

Figure 66   Tables for jumping off that nest together for easy storage.

A	V	T	F	G
J	B	I	H	S
W	K	E	C	V
L	D	M	N	R
X	Y	O	P	Q

1	7	0	9	1
2	4	3	8	0
6	3	2	5	7
8	5	1	6	4
4	9	3	2	5

a	l	u	h	i
m	b	g	k	j
n	o	u	f	t
w	c	p	q	r
d	x	e	s	z

Figure 67 Number and letter grids can be used for many activities.

Cardboard cutouts in geometric shapes of different sizes, such as circles, triangles, diamonds, squares, and concentric circles, provide targets for confined game spaces. They also reinforce pattern recognition. (See Figure 68.)

A grid on the ground of the type illustrated in Figure 69 is useful in letter discrimination and can be used for stay-on-the-line tag games. Every letter in the alphabet can be found in this pattern. Grids for figure discrimination can also be made.

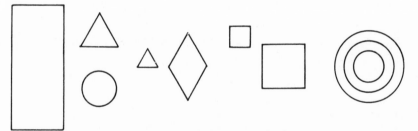

Figure 68 Cardboard cutouts.

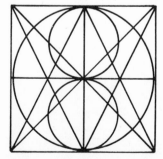

Figure 69 A letter-discrimination grid.

9

Sample Lessons

Movement activity sessions can be planned as part of regular outside time several days a week, or as a special group time in midmorning. Just prior to snack is a good time for movement sessions. Group sizes will vary depending on staffing capabilities and needs and the activity chosen. All lessons should begin with about two minutes of warm-up, move on to a vigorous activity, and then slow back down to cool the body off gradually for another two minutes at the end of the session. The total time for each of these lessons is about fifteen minutes.

SAMPLE LESSON 1

Theme: Being Airborne
Skill development: jumping for height and distance, muscle strength, eye-hand coordination, cardiovascular endurance
Equipment: rope tied between two trees or poles at a height of 5 ', cloth strips hanging down to different heights (between 4 ' and 5½ ') from the floor (See Figure 70.)
Teacher observation pointers: Check jump and landing techniques, extension of arm reach for streamers, running skills.

A. Warm-up
Group warm-up with "Can You?" imagery challenges. Can you

stretch like a cat waking up?
wiggle your toes as if someone were tickling you?
walk like a duck?

Figure 70 Cloth strips hanging from rope between two trees used for a jumping game.

B. Rope Jump (Reach It)

Divide the group in two, half about ten feet in front of the rope and half on the side watching. Have the first half run together and try to reach the streamers. After this group has had its turn, the other group goes. Repeat several times.

Variations:

1. Ask the children for suggestions.
2. In one long line at the end of the rope, have the children run and jump, trying to reach each streamer in succession. Return from the opposite side.
3. Vary the distance the children run before jumping.
4. Divide the group into pairs and have each child determine which streamer is too easy, too hard, or just right for jumping.

C. Popcorn Game (See page 100.)

D. Cooling down

Slow stretching challenges. Can you

be as tall as you can?
be as small as you can?
sway in a gentle breeze?

SAMPLE LESSON 2

Theme: Balloons in Flight
Skill development: catching, eye-hand coordination, flexibility
Equipment: balloons, tires or hoops for targets
Teacher observation pointers: Check whether eyes follow the
  balloon at all times.

A. Warm-up

Group warm-up with "Can You?" imagery challenges. Can you

> circle your arms like a slow airplane propeller? (Gradually
> increase speed until arm movements make children
> move around the room. Slow down as if to come in for
> a landing.)
>
> follow an imaginary bouncing ball? (First use only the
> eyes, then head, then upper body, then whole body.
> Reverse until only the eyes are used.)

B. Balloons Up

Every child is given a balloon. The goal is to bat it into the air and
keep it up as long as possible. Experiment, using different parts
of the body to keep it in the air.

C. Balloon Targets

Spread tires and hoops over the floor. Starting at one end of the
room, each child bats the balloon through the air to a target and
bats it in.
  Variations:

1. Limit batting to a specific body part.
2. Vary the movement pattern to the target.
3. Try to bounce the balloon to the target.

D. Partner Batting

Children choose a partner. On the signal "Go," partners bat the
balloon back and forth between themselves as they run to a
designated spot and back.

Increase the size of the group moving one balloon until all the children are working as one group.

E. Cooling down
Mirrors (See page 54.)

SAMPLE LESSON 3

Theme: Fast and Slow
Skill development: locomotor skills, auditory processing, flexibility, directionality
Equipment: rhythm instrument; steps, benches, or jumping tables
Teacher observation pointers: Note locomotor pattern characteristics of children.

A. Warm-up
Rolling: Log Rolls, Forward Rolls, Egg Rolls (See page 89.)

B. Rhythm Walk
Beat out a simple rhythm and have children walk around the space without touching anyone. Then change the beat so there is a clear variation in speed. Have children walk as fast as they can with the first beat, as slowly as they can with the other.
   Variations:

1. Move from walking to running, leaping, or jumping.
2. Vary the directions: move forward, backward, to the right, to the left.
3. Let the children form groups and make up rhythms by hand-clapping. Have them vary the movement in their groups.

C. Safe Tag (See page 64.)
Play the game as described, but allow the person who is "It" to decide the speed. For instance, "It" may have everyone run fast or slowly, or "It" can walk fast while the others jump slowly.

D. Cooling down
Have children move according to the rhythm beat, which should

be quick at the beginning and get progressively slower and slower and slower.

SAMPLE LESSON 4

Theme: Stopping and Starting
Skill development: locomotor patterns, auditory processing, cardiovascular endurance, reaction time, agility
Equipment: noise maker like whistle
Teacher observation pointers: Note locomotor pattern characteristics of children.

A. Warm-up
Group warm-up with "Can You?" imagery challenges. Can you

       run slowly?
       run as though your feet were in sticky gum?
       walk carefully so as not to pop any bubbles?

B. Whistle Run
When the children hear one whistle blast from the teacher, they run. When they hear two blasts, they stop. Use a designated section in the play area to run in.
    Variations:

1. Run holding hands with a partner.
2. Change the movement pattern.
3. Have all the children run. When one stops, they all must stop. No one can move again until everyone has stopped.

C. Freeze Tag (See page 62.)

D. Cooling down
Slow stretching challenges. Can you

       walk around wiggling your arms, legs, fingers, and head?
       stretch as tall as a tree?
       stretch down to the ground.
       spread out as wide as your body can?

be as skinny as you can?
roll around at your waist without moving your feet?

SAMPLE LESSON 5

Theme: Stability
Skill development: balance, body-part identification, flexibility
Equipment: none
Teacher observation pointers: Note the relationship of the body to the ground (the lower the body, the greater the stability) and check for widening of the base of support.

A. Warm-up
Group warm-up with "Can You?" imagery challenges. Can you

make your body as wide as possible and walk around the room keeping yourself very wide?
sit across from a partner holding hands and touching feet?
rock gently forward and back, side to side, in a circle?
try to stand by pushing against each other's feet and pulling up together?

B. Points (See page 51.)

C. Ships in the Harbor (See page 64.)

D. Cooling Down
Can you

find a position from which your body can be easily knocked over?
find another position with a partner?

(In both instances guide children with questions so they end up very low to the ground.)

APPENDIX:
Observation Checklists

SUGGESTED REFERENCES

INDEX

Appendix:
Observation Checklists

Duplicate these lists every few weeks to record the observations you make of the children. To use them, check the appropriate description for each child. By looking for the strengths and weaknesses of individual children and the class as a whole, you can use these checklists to plan activity sessions.

Observation Checklist: Walking
(Date _____)

	Name of Child				
Skill Level					

Arm action
  High-guard position
  Straight, swung at sides					

Knee Action
  Exaggerated bend during walk
  Smooth action as leg lifts off ground					

Hip rotation
  No rotation
  Some rotation
  Full rotation, first toward the back to
    support the forward leg and then forward
    as weight shifts					

Base of support
  Feet wide apart (wide base)
  Feet close together (narrow base)					

Stride length
  Short
  Moderate					

Foot contact
  Flat
  Heel-toe
  Toes out
  Toes in
  Toes straight ahead					

Rhythm
  Choppy, uneven
  Smooth					

Notes:

Observation Checklist: Running
(Date _____)

	Name of Child				
Skill Level					
Arm action Straight, little movement Swung freely sideways across diagonal body Swung in opposition to leg movement					
Leg action Knee moved out to side, then forward Knee lifted high, heel moved close to buttocks					
Foot action Flat foot Push-off on balls of feet Weight on whole foot Weight on ball of foot Toes pointed out Toes pointed in Toes pointed straight					
Trunk Straight Some backward lean Some forward lean					
Stride length Short Increased length					
Running speed Slow and deliberate Increasing speed					
Control Stops and starts with ease with difficulty Changes direction with ease with difficulty					

Notes:

Observation Checklist: Jumping
(Date _____)

Skill Level	Name of Child				
Steps down one foot to other					
Steps down one foot to two feet					
Jumps down two feet to two feet					
Leaps (runs and jumps from one foot to other)					
Jumps forward two feet to two feet					
Runs and jumps forward one foot to two feet					
Jumps over object two feet to two feet					

Notes:

Observation Checklist: Vertical Jump (Using a Target)
(Date _____)

	Name of Child				
Skill Level					

Arm action
  Held up to side
  Swung out to back
  Forced up					

Hip and leg action
  Minimal crouch (knees and hips bent slightly)
  Too deep crouch (knees and hips bent
    deeply)
  Effective crouch (knees and hips bent about
    45 degrees)					

Foot action
  One-foot takeoff and landing
  Two-foot takeoff and landing combination
  One-foot takeoff with two-foot landing or
    two-foot takeoff with one-foot landing					

In air
  Hips and knees bent
  Body straight, hips and knees extended					

Notes:

Observation Checklist: Standing Long Jump
(Date _____)

	Name of Child					
Skill Level						

Arm action
   Up in high-guard position
   Held back as jump is made
   Thrust forward and up						

Hip and knee action
   Minimal crouch (knees and hips bent
     slightly)
   Too deep crouch (knees and hips bent
     deeply)
   Effective crouch (knees and hips bent, about
     45 degrees)						

Foot action
   One-foot takeoff and landing
   Two-foot takeoff and landing combination
   One-foot takeoff with two-foot landing or
     two-foot takeoff with one-foot landing						

In air
   Body not extended, hips and knees already
     bent for landing
   Body extended, then hips and knees bent for
     landing						

Landing
   Uncontrolled
   Controlled						

Notes:

Observation Checklist: Throwing
(Date _____)

	Name of Child				
Skill Level					
Stage 1 Feet stationary Ball held near ear and pushed straight down No hip rotation No step as ball is released					
Stage 2 Minimal rotation to side opposite throwing arm Ball behind head, cocked in hand					
Stage 3 Step forward to foot on same side as throwing arm					

Stage 4
Steps to opposite foot
Trunk rotated to opposite side
Weight shifted from side with ball to
    opposite side as child steps with throw
Ball released with whip-like motion
Follow-through with hand in direction
    of target					

Notes:

Observation Checklist: Catching
(Date _____)

	Name of Child				
Skill Level					
Stage 1 Arms held straight out, palms up Traps ball against chest Claps at ball Uses vise grip on ball Head turned to side Leans away from ball					
Stage 2 Arms in front, elbows bent Arms encircling ball at chest, robot-like					
Stage 3 Ball bounced on chest, then controlled with arms					

Stage 4
Hands positioned according to flight of ball
Gives way to force of ball by bending at
    hips and knees
Continues to give way by moving in
    same direction as path of ball					

Notes:

Observation Checklist: Kicking
(Date _____)

	Name of Child				
Skill Level					
Initial kicking Pushes ball with shins while running					

Stage 1
  Leg straight while kicking
  Leg moved up and forward at ball contact
  No accompanying body movement					

Stage 2 Lower leg lifted behind to prepare for kick					

Stage 3
  Upper leg brought back, knee bent
  Increased arc of kick
  Some body adjustments
  Leg overcocked					

Stage 4
  Back trunk lean
  Arm and body adjusted during follow-
    through
  Moves farther behind ball in preparation
  Moves total body into kick					

Contact with the ball
  Kicks *through* the ball
  Kicks *at* the ball					

Notes:

Observation Checklist: Climbing
(Date _____)

	Name of Child					
Skill Level						
Foot action						
Marks time going up steps						
Marks time going down steps						
Uses alternating foot pattern going up steps						
going down steps						
Hand action						
Uses hands in hand-over-hand manner						
Slides hands along						
Unsure of hand placement						
Body position						
Faces direction of movement						
Turned toward object being climbed						

Notes:

Suggested References

Capon, J. *Perceptual Motor Development Series*. Belmont, Ca.,: Fearon-Pitman Publishers, 1975. (Includes *Balance Activities*; *Ball, Rope, Hoop Activities*; *Basic Movement Activities*; *Beanbag, Rhythm-Stick Activities*; and *Tire, Parachute Activities*.)

Corbin, C. (ed.). *A Textbook of Motor Development*. Dubuque, Iowa: William C. Brown Co., 1973.

Espenscade, A. S., and Eckert, H. M. *Motor Development*. 2nd ed. Columbus, Ohio: Charles Merrill Publishing Co., 1980.

Kamii, C., and DeVries, R. *Group Games in Early Education: Implications of Piaget's Theory*. Washington, D.C.: National Association for the Education of Young Children, 1980. ·

Mosston, M. *Teaching Physical Education: From Command to Discovery*. Columbus, Ohio: Charles Merrill Publishing Co., 1966.

Ridenour, M. V. (ed.). *Motor Development: Issues and Applications*. Princeton, N.J.: Princeton Book Co., 1978.

Wickstrom, R. *Fundamental Motor Patterns*. 2nd ed. Philadelphia: Lea & Febiger, 1977.

Index

An italicized number indicates a figure or table appears on that page.

Adventure playground, 107
Agility, 40, 64, 68, 76, 87, 121
Airborne: as theme of Sample
  Lesson 1, 117–18
American Adventure Play Associ-
  ation, 108
Animal Walks, 91
Auditory discrimination, 41, 55, 63,
  75, 85, 99, 100, 120, 121

Balance, 34–36, 51, 53, 56, 58, 62,
  64, 79, 84, 122; games, 88–89;
  general principles of, 36; posture
  and, 40
Balance beams, 88–89, 111, *112*
Balance boards, 88–89, 111–13, *112*
Ball balancing, 81
Ball-bouncing, 90
Balloon Jumpers, 67
Balloons, 71; in flight as theme of
  Sample Lesson 2, 119
Ball Pass, 72–73, *72, 73*
Balls, 81–82, 90; games for throwing
  and catching, 70–75, *71*; making
  yarn and sock, 110, *110*
Ball skills, 7
Bean bags, 51, 71, 74, 87, 110, 114
Bear Walk, 91, *92*
Bicycle inner tubes, 96, 111
Blankets, 96, 113

Body image. *See* Body parts and
  body image
Body Outline Drawings, 56
Body-Part Puzzles, 56–57, *57, 58*
Body parts and body image, 51–61,
  87; as perceptual motor com-
  ponent, 40; in Sample Lesson 5,
  122
Body-Part Walkabouts, 60–61, *60*
Body proportions, 8
Bouncing Ball, 90
Building Blocks, 86

"Can You?" Challenges: in body
  image and body parts, 51; in
  running, 61; in walking, 66; in
  throwing and catching, 70–71; in
  kicking, 75–76; with hoops and
  tires, 82, *83*; with ropes, 85; with
  bean bags, 87; with balance beams,
  88; with balance board, 89; stressing movement qualities, 97–99; in
  sample lessons, 117, 118, 121, 122
Cardiovascular endurance, 39, 61,
  75, 77, 83, 84, 87, 100, 121
Catching, 9, *27, 28–30*; as fundamental motor pattern, 26–29;
  games, 70–75; with bean bags, 87;
  in Sample Lesson 2, 119; Observation Checklist for, 132

Checklists, Observation, 125–34
Climbing, 9, 31–34, *33, 35*; "marking time" in, 33; stairs, 34; ladders, 34; Observation Checklist for, 134
Cloth strips, 117
Color Run, 63
Command: in Mosston's teaching style, 43
Competition: in games, 47
Cooperation: in games, 46
Coordination, 8, 40, 53, 56, 76, 91, 96; in walking, 11; in running, 12
Crab Walk, 93, *93*
Crazy Legs, 77, *77*
Creativity, 2, 3; Mosston's approach to, 43; in playgrounds, 107, 108
Crossing the Stream, 68, *69*
Cutouts, cardboard, 115, *115*

Developmental schedules, 7, 9; age-ability norms and, 10; sequence in jumping and, 14; stages in throwing and, 22–26
DeVries, R., 42, 135
Directionality, 40, 54, 56, 60, 64, 87, 90, 91, 120
Disabled children, 10

Egg Roll, 89; in Sample Lesson 3, 120
Elephant Walk, 93
Environmental/structural components, 41, 49
Equipment, 71, 81, 96; in environmental/structural components, 41; making and buying of, 108–15. *See also* Balance beams; Balance boards; Balls; Bean bags; Hoops; Mat activities; Ropes
Exercise, 103, 104
Eye-foot coordination, 41, 76, 77, 78, 79, 87
Eye-hand coordination, 40, 54, 67, 70, 72, 73, 74, 75, 76, 81, 86, 87, 90, 109, 119

Figure-ground discrimination, 40, 115
Flexibility, 39, 51, 53, 54, 56, 58, 67, 86, 90, 91, 119, 120, 122
Force, use of, in movement qualities, 41
Form perception, 40, 56, 60
Freeze Tag, 62–63; in Sample Lesson 4, 121
Frog Jump, 93, *94*
Fundamental motor patterns, 7, 61–79, 100; progression of development of, 9; children with special needs, 10

Go Tag, 64, *65*
Gravity, 7
Grids, number and letter, 114, *115*
Group size: in environmental/structural components, 41; in Mosston's teaching style, 43
Growth, physical, 8
Guided discovery: in Mosston's teaching style, 43

Handicapped. *See* Disabled children
Health, 103
Heart, 103–104; and pulse rate, 103, *104*
Height, 8
Helpful hints: in running, 61; in jumping, 66; in catching, 70; in throwing, 70
High-guard position: in walking, 11, *11*
Hit the Clown, 73
Hoop or Tire Tag, 84
Hoops, 52, 71, 119; games with, 82–85, *83*; making, 108, *108*. *See also* Tires
Hopping, 13

Imagery, 97, 117, 118, 119, 121, 122
Individual program: in Mosston's teaching style, 43
Insiders, 83, *84*
Instructional components, 41, 49

Jumping, 9, *18, 19, 20, 21, 22,* 83, 86, 100; as fundamental motor pattern, 13–22; variations—hopping, leaping, 13; developmental sequence of, 14; height increases in, 17; "winging out" action in, 22; games, 66–69; Observation Checklist for, 128. *See also* Standing Long Jump; Vertical Jump
Jumping tables, 113, *114;* in Sample Lesson 3, 120

Kamii, C., 42, 135
Kicking, 9, *30, 31, 32;* as fundamental motor pattern, 29–31; games, 75–79; Observation Checklist for, 133
Kinesthesis, 40, 90

Ladders, 113, *114*
Lame Puppy Walk, 93, *95*
Language, development of, 7
Laterality, 40, 51, 54, 56, 60, 87, 91
Leap Frog, 68
Leaping, 13
Letter grids, 114, *115*
Locomotor patterns, 41; in Sample Lesson 3, 120; in Sample Lesson 4, 121
Log Roll, 89; in Sample Lesson 3, 120

Machines, 53, *53*
Mainstreaming, 10
Marking time: in climbing stairs, 33; in climbing ladders, 34
Mat activities, 89–95
Mirrors, 54, *55;* in Sample Lesson 2, 120
Mosston, M., 43–44, 135
Motor development: motor abilities and, 7; physical maturation and, 10; framework of, 39. *See also* Fundamental motor patterns
Motor skills, 7
Movement education, 44–45

Movement exploration, 44
Movement patterns: locomotor, 41; non-locomotor, 41
Movement qualities, 41; use of time in, 41; use of space in, 41; use of force in, 41; "Can You?" challenges in, 97; in Sample Lesson 3, 120
Mulberry Bush, 100
Muscle strength, 39, 67, 68
Muscle tissue, 8
Muscular endurance, 39
Musical Hoops, 85
Myelin, 8
Myelinization, 8

Neuromotor, 40
Non-locomotor patterns, 41, 89
Number grids, 114, *115*

Observation Checklists, 125–34
Observation hints, 36–37
Obstacle courses, 95, *96*
One Step, 87
One, Two, Button My Shoe, 63
Outcome, movement, 37

Parachute, 113
Pattern recognition, 85, 115
Perceptual/motor skills, 40, 68, 70
Performance: changes in, 8, 9; boy-girl differences in, 10
Physical components, 39–41, 49
Physical fitness, 39
Physical growth, 8
Playgrounds, 107–108; adventure, 107
Play yards, 107–108; yard markings in, 108
Points, 51–52, *52*
Popcorn Game, 100, 118
Posture, 40
Problem-solving skills, 2, 3; in games, 42; in Mosston's teaching style, 43–44
Puppy Walk, 91

Rabbit Hop, 93, *94*
Reachers, 86
Reach It. *See* Rope Jump
Reaction time, 40, 62, 63, 121
Reciprocal teaching: in Mosston's
  teaching style, 43
Rhythm: in walking, 11, 97; in
  Sample Lesson 3, 120
Roly-Poly, 91
Rope Jump (Reach It), 118, *118*
Rope Kickers, 78, *78*
Ropes, 52, 71, 85–86, 109, 117, 118
Running, 9, *14, 15, 16, 17,* 74, 83,
  84, 85, 117; as fundamental motor
  pattern, 12–13; games, 61–65;
  Observation Checklist for, 127

Safe Tag, 64; in Sample Lesson 3,
  120
Safety, 105. *See also* Health
Sample Lessons, 117–22
Schedules, developmental. *See* De-
  velopmental schedules
Scoops, 96, 109, *109*
Scooter Boards, 96, 111
Seal Walk, 91, *92*
Seat Circle, 89
Sequencing, 41, 90, 95, 99, 100
Sex differences: in performance, 10;
  in throwing, 22, 24
Shadow Games, 58, *59*
Ships in the Harbor, 64; in Sample
  Lesson 5, 122
Simon Says, 55
Slithery Snake, 90, *91*
Snuffers, 79
Socialization, 7
Songs, traditional movement, 101
Space, use of, in movement quali-
  ties, 41
Spatial orientation, 40, 56, 60, 64,
  82, 83, 84, 85, 86, 90, 91
Special needs, children with, 10
Speed, 8, 40, 62, 63, 64; in running,
  13

Squares, foam rubber or carpet, 109,
  109
Stability: in walking, 11; in Sample
  Lesson 5, 122
Stairs, 113, *113*
Standing Long Jump, 17, 19, *19, 20;*
  Observation Checklist for, 130.
  See also Jumping
Stand Up, 56
Stethoscope, 104
Stilts, tin can, 110, *111*
Stop Ball, 75
Stopping and starting: in Freeze Tag,
  62; in Sample Lesson 3, 121
Streamers, 96
Strength, 8, 85, 86, 90, 91, 96, 100;
  in running, 12; in jumping, 66
Stunts, 89–90
Success, 2, 3; in games, 42

Target cutouts, *74,* 113
Task: in Mosston's teaching style, 43
Teaching, reciprocal, 43
Thread the Needle, 90
Throwers and Catchers, 74
Throwing, 9, *23, 24, 25, 26,* 81–82;
  as fundamental motor pattern,
  22–26; games, 70–75, *71, 74;* Ob-
  servation Checklist for, 131
Tiger Hunt, Going on a, 99
Time: use of, in movement qualities,
  41; in environmental/structural
  components, 41; fast/slow, as
  theme of Sample Lesson 3, 120
Tires, 71, 82–85, 111, 119. *See also*
  Hoops
Traffic cones, 110
Turk Stand, 90

Vertical Jump, 20, *20, 21, 22;* Observation Checklist for, 128. *See also*
  Jumping

Walking, 7, 9, *11, 12, 13;* as fundamental motor pattern, 10–12;

games, 65–66; Observation Check-
list for, 126
Wallopers, 76
Weight, 8
Whistle Run, 121
Wickstrom, R., 9, *11, 14, 19, 20, 24,
27, 30,* 135
Wring the Dish Rag, 90

Yard markings, 114; number and letter grids as, 114, *115*